D1712915

Law Firm Mergers

Law Firm Mergers

Taking a Strategic Approach

Giles Rubens and Hildebrandt International

First published 2005 by
PALGRAVE MACMILLAN
Houndmills, Basingstoke, Hampshire RG21 6XS and
175 Fifth Avenue, New York, N. Y. 10010
Companies and representatives throughout the world

PALGRAVE MACMILLAN is the global academic imprint of the Palgrave Macmillan division of St. Martin's Press, LLC and of Palgrave Macmillan Ltd. Macmillan® is a registered trademark in the United States, United Kingdom and other countries. Palgrave is a registered trademark in the European Union and other countries.

ISBN 1–4039–0315–8 hardback

This book is printed on paper suitable for recycling and made from fully managed and sustained forest sources.

A catalogue record for this book is available from the British Library.

Library of Congress Cataloging-in-Publication Data
Ruben, Giles.
    Law firm mergers : taking a strategic approach / Giles Rubens and Hildebrandt International.
        p. cm.
    Includes bibliographical references and index.
    ISBN 1–4039–0315–8 (cloth)
        1. Law firms–Mergers–United States. I. Hildebrandt International (Firm) II. Title.
KF315.R83 2004
340′.068–dc22   2004051236

10   9   8   7   6   5   4   3   2   1
14   13   12   11   10   09   08   07   06   05

Printed and bound in Great Britain by
Antony Rowe Ltd, Chippenham and Eastbourne

Contents

List of Figures

Acknowledgement

First I would like to thank my many colleagues and friends at Hildebrandt International who have supported and assisted in the planning and writing of this book; in particular Julia Hayhoe and Robert Ashing in developing the initial idea and structure and also other members of the London office who have each provided highly valuable support and help.

Secondly I wish to thank the many clients I have worked with over the years who have provided both motivation and experiences for this book.

Lastly a big thank you to my immediate family – Alison, Oliver and Clemmie for putting up with me during the writing of this book.

To all of you – a sincere thank you.

Giles Rubens

Introduction

Purpose of book

The purpose of this book, intended for partners and others in senior management positions in mid-size to large law firms, is four-fold:

(i)   to assist such firms decide whether they should consider merger;
(ii) to guide firms that decide to merge through the process of identifying a suitable partner;
(iii) to provide guidelines to undertaking successful merger negotiations;
(iv) to help ensure that firms do realise the anticipated benefits of merger through effective post-merger integration.

This book contains numerous checklists, practical tips and analytical methodologies. It is not, however, primarily intended as a 'how to' guide; that is a secondary aim. Its primary aim is to provide a framework based on sound strategic principles to guide firms through the process of considering merger.

The fundamental premise underlying this book is that merger is a means to an end, not an end itself; it follows, therefore, that merger should only be pursued if:

(i)   there are in existence clear strategic objectives;
(ii) merger is demonstrably the most effective way of achieving these;
(iii) there is a strong commitment to implementing the necessary post-merger integration in order that the merger achieves the aims identified.

In practice, not all mergers follow the type of structured framework outlined in this book: many mergers occur whose origins can be traced back to more opportunistic circumstances such as historical ties between two firms, a chance meeting or a long term friendship between senior partners or an approach relatively out of the blue from one firm to another. Such circumstances may arise without, necessarily, significant structured strategic evaluation having occurred in advance. By attempting, however, to keep each chapter as self-contained as possible and by providing a brief synopsis of each, the aim is to make the book as valuable to those firms perhaps already part way down the track of considering (or even negotiating) merger as to those firms that are essentially entering this territory from scratch for the first time.

While the book is primarily focused on genuine mergers, hopefully it is also of relevance to those pursuing 'bolt-on' opportunities or even takeovers, as the primary issues involved do have a large degree of overlap.

Background and aims

Survey after survey in recent years in both Europe and the US has highlighted the high levels of interest among law firms in merger, with very few firms indicating that it has no part in their strategic thinking and increasing numbers stating that they are either actively considering merger and/or would respond with genuine interest to an approach from another firm.

The high level of interest in merger is reflected in the actual levels of merger activity and while there is nothing new about law firm merger there are increasing numbers of mergers occurring despite some evidence of a slight slowdown in merger activity in recent years. These mergers cover the broadest spectrum of practices ranging from the highest and most profitable firms seeking, most often, to extend their geographic coverage, to the smallest single city or town practices seeking to increase their critical mass or develop their breadth of capability within an existing location or simply to address issues of succession.

Despite the high levels of interest in merger and indeed the high levels of merger activity there remain significant variations in the outcome of mergers. Some, unquestionably, have been successful and others unquestionably have failed – sometimes ultimately leading to dissolution, break-up or takeover. Many others can be considered, most fairly, neither successes nor failures; they have resulted in larger firms being created but not obviously better or more competitive ones.

It is, of course, impossible to predict with certainty at the outset which mergers will be successful and which will not. It is, however, possible to increase the likelihood of success significantly and that is an aim of this book.

A fair amount has been written about law firm merger in the past but the focus of much of this is very largely 'case study' based or covering the mechanics of merger – 'how to do' texts. Little has been written covering the principles of merger and this is the intention and focus here:

- Why should firms consider merger?
- What is the rationale for merger?
- What conditions underpin successful merger?
- What should be the focus of merger discussions?
- What helps ensure that the identified benefits of a merger are realised in practice?

Inevitably a principles-based approach cannot cover every eventuality nor every set of circumstances. Neither can it provide 'universal answers'. What it can do, however, is provide a framework to assist those considering merger (or who have been approached by another practice proposing exploring the potential of merger). Even in a principles-based text, however, there are limitations and there is inevitably a huge difference between the circumstances surrounding merger between, say, leading firms in differing Jurisdictions that are seeking to build international capability and two local practices seeking to merge.

The principles explored in this book are not, however, purely theoretical. Over the past 30 years, Hildebrandt International, whose many consultants have contributed to this book, has advised on more law firm mergers than any other organisation. The majority of these mergers have been successful although not all. Irrespective, however, of success or otherwise, lessons have been learnt from each merger and these 'lessons' provide a complementary empirical balance to the principles and frameworks. There is, therefore, an enormously strong underlying body of practical experience and this has been used to attempt above all else to be pragmatic at all times.

No doubt we have failed in these aims at points and we also have no doubt that there are other shortcomings in this text. Please let us know of these by contacting us at mergerbook@hildebrandt.com.

This will not only help us develop our thinking on the topic but will also allow us to provide further ideas – either through future editions and/or on our website.

Structure

This book is divided into three main sections and as far as possible the sections and each chapter within each are discrete and stand-alone.

Part I reviews the impact of competition on the legal market and the role merger can play in supporting firms achieve their strategic objectives. It also outlines a framework for identifying potential merger candidates in broad terms.

Part II outlines the key steps in a merger and the considerations at each of these; it explores the principles of preparing for merger, developing a business case, conducting negotiations and due diligence.

Part III explores the issues of post-merger integration and the steps that need to be taken to help ensure that the potential benefits of merger are indeed realised.

Lastly it is important to mention what is not covered in this text and there are two areas in particular that have been omitted:

- First, detailed accounting and tax issues are not dealt with and there are two reasons for this: in part because they are major issues and hence outside the scope of this book, particularly when one takes into account that they vary hugely from jurisdiction to jurisdiction, but there are also issues here in that the accounting and tax issues are changing all the time and hence any attempt at coverage carries a high risk of becoming out of date and, potentially, significantly and dangerously so.
- Secondly, the issue of what structure a merged firm might consider to practise under is also not covered. Again, this is an extensive and complex issue covered by a myriad of differing bar and other regulations on a jurisdiction by jurisdiction basis and also subject to changes from time to time with limited indication of convergence of the differing rules and regulations.

Given the complexity of each of these issues and the changes occurring in the options open to merging firms we can do no better than repeat the recommendations so favoured by legal practitioners – seek up-to-date professional advice!

Synopsis of Chapters

Part I   Competition, strategy and the role of merger

Chapter 1 outlines trends in the legal market and highlights the importance of firms having a clear strategic focus; it also identifies the characteristics and capabilities that firms need to develop to support their long term success.

Chapter 2 explores the role merger can play in supporting firms achieve their strategic objectives arguing that firms should consider merger only when such a move is clearly the best (or only) way of achieving such objectives.

Part II   Preparing for merger

Chapter 3 summarises the steps firms should take to assess whether merger is an appropriate route forward and to identify a suitable merger partner; it also emphasises the importance of addressing identified shortcomings in one's own firm prior to pursuing merger.

Chapter 4 describes the process of assessing the strength of the business case for merger with the identified preferred firm – a critical but frequently only superficially addressed step.

Chapter 5 discusses the key steps in negotiating a merger and the importance for both parties of undertaking thorough due diligence.

Part III   Achieving post-merger integration

Chapter 6 focuses on the critical importance of developing and achieving commitment to a post-merger integration plan. The importance of managing expectations of what merger will deliver and the implications for partners is emphasised. It also discusses managing the post-merger integration process and ensuring that the identified benefits of merger are realised within the planned timescales.

Part I

Competition, Strategy and the Role of Merger

1
Trends in the Legal Market

Across the major more developed legal markets in the world, similar trends are apparent with the differences between jurisdictions more often related to timing and detail than to significant substance. Thus in the US, Western Europe, the more developed markets in South East Asia, Australia and Canada, there is a broadly similar restructuring occurring and with a continuing move towards a global market in professional services, it is realistic to assume that, subject to an absence of state or bar level imposed restrictions on competition and the freedom to practise, over time these trends will impact on other major economies such as Central and Eastern Europe, the South American markets, and so on.

These trends, in part demand side (client) driven and in part originating from the supply side (provider), are resulting in a fundamental restructuring of the marketplace and they create the environment which has resulted in such significant interest in merger.

Growing client sophistication

The first and perhaps most significant trend and driver of change is the growing sophistication of clients as buyers of legal services. In most jurisdictions it is only necessary to go back 25 years at the most to find a market where the providers of legal services (the law firms) were very much the dominant force; they tended to dictate the terms of the relationship and, in the main, high levels of deference towards the professions in general and lawyers in particular were the norm. Clients in the main were relatively inexperienced in

3

terms of buying legal services – perhaps even positively naïve compared to today – and with little in the way of practical guidance found it difficult to evaluate the quality of the services they received or to differentiate between alternative service providers. Information on firms was basic or, often the case, non-existent, advertising either prohibited or restricted to such an extent that it provided no assistance in selecting firms and the ubiquitous legal directories – that today more or less accurately cover the major jurisdictions with tier rankings of firms and their practices – had not even being dreamt of. Furthermore, the very concept of competition between law firms was not seen as an issue and effectively outside the consideration of the profession: the prevailing thinking being that 'all lawyers are equally qualified professionally, and therefore, by definition, equally qualified and competent to handle matters on which they are instructed'.

Although in some markets vestiges of these conditions remain, in most they have all but disappeared and today's buyers of legal services are hugely experienced and highly sophisticated in their purchasing. This change has occurred for a number of reasons with economic downturns often acting as something of a catalyst or 'accelerator' in terms of encouraging or even necessitating law firms to compete more aggressively for both new and existing clients and instructions, either on the basis of superior service or fees or some combination of the two. While recession or economic downturn has often been the catalyst, the 'drivers' of change have been clients' growing recognition through experience and greater transparency – a consequence of increasing levels of information about the market and about firms – that not all law firms are equal nor for that matter are all legal services of equal importance and hence perceived value.

These two factors working together created a momentum that has driven fundamental restructuring. At the heart of the market change has been the recognition by clients that not all legal services are of equal value and while historically, clients had been prepared to pay for services essentially on the basis of the 'time on the clock' or scale fees this has increasingly become an anachronism. In place clients have become increasingly prepared to pay for legal services only on the basis of the value that they perceive and judge has been delivered to their organisation or business or to themselves as private clients. Such clients continue to be prepared to pay premium rates for certain services but essentially this has become more and more restricted to what is perhaps best described as 'bet-the-company' matters and unfortunately, as far as law firms are concerned, there is a decreasing percentage of most clients' matters – be they corporate clients or private individuals – that fall into this category. Figure 1.1 illustrates the Value Pyramid. This shows the relative position of different types of work on the value pyramid and the inverse relationship between the perceived value of work (from the client perspective) and its price sensitivity.

Over time increasing proportions of work have become regarded as mid or low value as compared to the high value 'bet-the-company' matters. This mid- and lower-value work is work that clients need to have undertaken but is not considered to be so critical that it justifies premium rates; furthermore a very wide range of legal services providers are seen to have more or less equal and fully adequate capabilities to undertake it; a substantively indistinguishable and undifferentiated capability in the perception of clients. Over time it is hardly surprising that this work has tended to command less high fees and price has played a more and more significant role in purchasing decisions.

There are of course added complexities here in that the same client may perceive broadly similar instructions from a legal

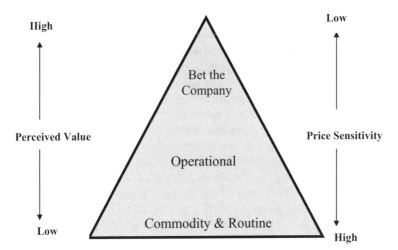

Figure 1.1 The Value Pyramid

perspective being of differing value dependent on, for example, the business context. So for example, two pieces of litigation or two corporate acquisitions, while of similar complexity and requiring a similar level of legal resource to complete, may have a very differing value attached to them from the same client's perspective. Furthermore, different clients may put differing values on exactly the same legal matter dependent on their perception of the value to them and, of course, their ability to pay. (For example, a leading international pharmaceutical corporate is likely to have deeper pockets to protect its Intellectual Property compared to a sparsely funded start-up bioscience company; objectively though it might be considered that the relative value and strategic importance of the IP to both clients falls into the 'bet-the-company' definition).

Law firm developments

The second factor driving change in the legal market has been the developments occurring inside law firms; this has been in part a response to the growing sophistication of clients but also a recognition by the most strategically minded and enlightened law firms that they neither wished to nor could service all parts of the market. These, more forward looking law firms, were the first to recognise three critical issues:

- first, that there was certain work that they particularly wanted to focus on – for many of the firms this meant the high level work for clients prepared and able to pay premium level fees and this was consistent with the aspirations of such firms to establish leading market positions at the 'top-end' of the market;
- second, that particular capabilities were required to develop and maintain a reputation as leaders and experts in such work. Strength in depth and genuine cutting edge technical expertise along with a highly commercial approach and exemplary service delivery were four such capabilities; these firms not only recognised the need for such capabilities but proceeded to build them so that they were able to deliver demonstrably superior services;
- third, that focusing on certain parts of the market and building the capabilities to be competitive there precluded these firms from competing for other work, either because of cost considerations (the

cost structure they carried to build competitiveness for the premium level work would result in them not being able to meet clients' pricing expectations around mid- and lower-value work and achieve an acceptable level of profit) or because they could not maintain the other competitive capabilities required within a firm that was primarily wishing to focus on higher value work.

In practice it was not only at the very top end of the market that this restructuring of law firms began (although it was particularly noticeable here) and in other areas law firms recognised that it was better to focus on certain types of clients or types of work (or some combination of the two) and service that supremely well rather than continue to attempt to be 'all things to all people'.

Thus over a relatively short period in most legal markets (say 5–10 years) a significant level of segmentational restructuring has occurred with something of a self reinforcing cycle developing.

Clients have reassessed the value of services according to the worth they perceive such services having and for the majority of services this has been downward. In addition, and as a consequence of the refocusing and restructuring occurring within law firms, clients have recognised that for differing legal services different law firms provide superior services and that while in certain circumstances it may be worthwhile to buy a bundle of services from a single provider even if that provider is not universally the 'best', there are limitations on how far such 'one-stop' purchasing is worth pursuing. It is not that clients are being promiscuous in their purchasing, as is sometimes claimed, especially by those who have found themselves losing clients and instructions, but that clients have recognised the greater value and other advantages that can be reaped by buying on a horses-for-courses basis.

Market restructuring

The outcome of these trends is apparent in all developed markets although there remain differences in detail. First there is clear segmentation. At the top end of each market (be it at a national or regional level within a jurisdiction) a small number of firms are competing for the highest value work – be it contentious or non-contentious or both – and this tends to be the premium level work of the most significant corporates, banks and the like. Beneath this are other tiers of firms, each seen as competitive for certain types of work or certain types of client (although not necessarily the types of work and client that those firms' partners would like to be seen as competitive for).

And this process of segmentation is occurring downward and across all jurisdictions. For most firms this has brought a level of discomfort as they have needed to restructure in order to develop genuine competitiveness in terms of servicing a part of the market. Greater discomfort however is being experienced by those firms that have either not recognised the need to refocus and restructure accordingly or have been unable to complete such a restructuring. For such firms, the outlook is bleak, as there is a high likelihood that successively in the areas that they practise in they will be perceived by the market as non-competitive compared to those firms that have focused on such areas and built superior service capabilities accordingly. Ultimately such firms are likely to find themselves on a downward cycle of losing their better quality clients and instructions, reducing margins and profit, and the loss of their best people. See Figure 1.2: The Downward Cycle of Losing Clients.

Work, inevitably and inexorably, migrates to the more competitive firms and so linked to this segmentation has been a concen-

Figure 1.2 The Downward Cycle of Losing Clients

tration on types of work and types of clients in particular practices. This has reached significant levels in the more developed markets with a smallish number of firms winning an increasing proportion of particular types of work and this can be seen across the market: at the premium end with 'bet-the-company' transactions, financing and litigation as well as at the lower value end of the market with insurance defence work, straightforward secured lending, routine conveyancing and the like.

Between the extremes of the high value 'bet-the-company' work and the low value 'commodity' work there is, of course, the mid-value work. However, much of this is being revalued over time as clients continue to reassess its worth and in the main such re-evaluation is downwards; this reduction in fees that clients are prepared to pay can become accelerated by aggressive or even predatory pricing by some law firms – especially common during economic periods when work volume is reduced or by firms simply trying to build (or maintain) volume and market share.

It would be wrong to assume that a complete polarisation will occur: there will continue to be a level of mid-value work – some of which at least will be previously high-value work that over time has been reassessed downwards. On the other hand, to perceive the mid-value sector as a safe haven for law firms where competition will be less severe or aggressive than in the high- or low-value sectors would be wrong. Here, as elsewhere in the market, clients will continue to exercise sophisticated buying of legal services, clear of the capabilities they require of their legal services providers and discerning in their selection accordingly.

So while there will remain mid-value work, there will also be many highly competent firms competing for it, including some who have been squeezed out of competing for the higher value work because of a perceived lack of competitiveness, others who are seeking to move away from the lower value commodity work, and, of course, a third group who have traditionally seen the mid-value market as their natural territory.

These two trends – growing client sophistication and refocusing/restructuring by law firms to develop competitiveness in particular areas – are driving huge changes in the marketplace and, without doubt, are leading many firms to consider where they wish to compete in the market in the future and the capabilities they need to build in order to be competitive in that position.

This is leading many firms to consider merger and we shall return to this point shortly.

International capability

In one part of the market, however, there is an additional consideration driving the thinking about merger and this is the need or otherwise for a global, international or at least multi-jurisdictional capability.

To compete for certain types of work – and in particular international M&A, Capital Markets and Litigation work there is no realistic chance of being a leading player without a significant geographic capability and while for a small number of firms it may be possible to provide such capability through a network or alliance of firms – possibly working on the so called 'best friends' basis – for the majority such an approach is not likely to meet the expectations of the very sophisticated purchasers of such services.

Hence there is an imperative in some firms to build an international or at least multi-jurisdictional capability to service the top end of the market and indeed other parts of the market that are international in nature. For some firms, setting up local practices and then building them through organic growth has been seen as the appropriate approach. Increasingly, however, this has become recognised as an inadequate approach because of the time taken to build overseas capabilities in this way and in it not providing the required capabilities (e.g. breadth and depth of expertise) for a considerable period of time to service international clients and instructions competitively. And so for some firms and in particular, but by no means exclusively, those wishing to compete at the very top end of the market developing an international capability in a relatively short timeframe is a further driver for merger.

Competing effectively in the restructured market

The restructuring in the marketplace, in part client led and in part service provider driven is forcing law firms to become far more focused in terms of where they wish to compete. This is forcing firms to make difficult decisions: first, to reorganise themselves away from an unrelated set of practices each addressing separate sectors of the market, replacing this with a coherent focus to their business based on clear synergies between both the practice groups and client segments being targeted. Secondly, firms are having to ensure that their internal systems and processes – including their remuneration structure – are genuinely supporting as opposed to being in conflict with the strategic focus.

There are, of course, a number of strategic options open to firms in terms of their specific focus and while there are just three broad strategic positionings that are valid, within each of these there are a number of variations:

- The first strategic positioning is based on building a full service but focused offering, with a higher value emphasis and targeted at specific segments of the market such as:
  - global transactions,
  - mid-market international clients/work,
  - mid-market domestic clients/work;
  or alternatively comprising a high value package of services focused on international or global clients.
- The second strategic positioning is based on focused specialisms, also with a mid- to higher value emphasis; this could be based on a single or limited number of practice areas offered to either a global or domestic client base. Alternatively, it might consist of a package of coherent specialisms offered to one or a limited number of defined client types.
- The third clear strategic positioning is essentially commodity or near commodity type work which by definition is lower value, and this too could be targeted either domestically or internationally.

As firms migrate to market positions along these lines and develop competitiveness accordingly, the pressure will build on the broader service generalist who will become increasingly regarded as 'offering everything to anybody but not renowned or expert at anything'; this will occur at both a local and national level. The outlook for such firms is not attractive.

Success is, however, far more complex than simply identifying and agreeing a valid strategic positioning; despite the challenges of achieving this, in reality this is the easy part!

Five dimensions for success

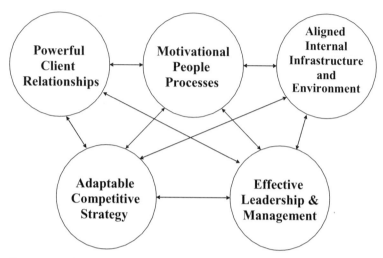

Figure 1.3   The Five Dimensions of Success

Figure 1.3 illustrates how successful firms of the future will also need to manage themselves effectively along five key dimensions and ensure both coherence and integration between all of these:

i)   adopt an adaptable, competitive strategy;
ii)   ensure effective leadership and management;
iii) maintain an aligned internal infrastructure and environment;
iv)   develop motivational people processes;
v)   build powerful client relationships.

Each of these key dimensions is elaborated below.

i)   An adaptable competitive strategy

As discussed above a fundamental keystone for success in the future is having a valid and competitive strategy to which there is a high level of commitment. This needs to define:

- the core clients the firm is seeking to service;
- the core practice areas and hence services it intends to offer;

- the value positioning of the firm (high, medium or low);
- the geographic coverage/capability.

There also needs to be clarity concerning how the firm will compete: how will it outperform other practices in a way that is relevant and attractive to clients and this is the critical 'competitive' element of a strategy. To have a strategy which defines the four elements listed immediately above, but which does not address the issue of competitiveness, is not an effective strategy.

As well as there being clarity concerning the key elements of the strategy, adaptability also needs to be built in; clients' needs and expectations change, competitors pursue new initiatives, new opportunities arise, the social, political, economic and commercial landscape alters, and so on. A strategy that cannot adapt to such changes will inevitably lead, sooner or later, to failure.

And this need for ensuring adaptability is one of the core responsibilities of the second keystone for success, namely effective leadership and management.

ii) Effective leadership and management

Developing a competitive strategy and ensuring that it remains responsive and adaptable to trends and changes in the market requires effective leadership and management. The key requirements of a firm's leadership and management are to provide vision and direction for the firm and, equally importantly, to ensure there is a sense of shared purpose; all of this needs translating both into clear long-term goals and short- and medium-term actions and targets. It is in driving the firm towards the achievement of these goals – strategic implementation – that the central focus of management lies, and an integral aspect of this is ensuring a strong focus on performance management, ensuring that performance across the firm – both of the lawyers and other fee earners and of those in the support function – is at a level commensurate and consistent with achieving the strategic goals.

The style and approach of this management will vary from firm to firm. In some firms it will be relatively centralised, in others less so; in some it will be formal and structured, in others informal and relatively unstructured. The key point is not how management occurs but that it does occur and that it is appropriate and effective for the circumstances; indeed it is likely to change from time to time, not least because of changes in those fulfilling leadership and management roles and the circumstances and challenges that the firm is facing at any one time.

Above all the role of leadership and management is to ensure that a high level of understanding of the competitive environment exists throughout the firm and that this is reflected in the strategy (to which there has to be high level of commitment).

iii)   Aligned internal infrastructure and environment

The third critical element of success is building and maintaining an internal environment that is aligned with, and supportive of, the achievement of the strategy. First, and probably most challengingly, it means ensuring that the behaviour and priorities of partners (and other lawyers) are directed at achieving the agreed strategic objectives – this is the ultimate test of transforming a strategy from there being commitment to it at a conceptual level to its practical implementation.

It also means ensuring that the firm's decision-making structure and processes are designed to assist the achievement of the strategy and as a key element of this that the decision-making process is timely, efficient and operates at all times within the context of achieving the firm's strategy. In a similar way the firm's systems, procedures, processes and technology all need to be aligned with the achievement of the firm's strategy and so too must its values and culture. Without this alignment a firm's strategy will most likely never be implemented and at best be partially implemented in an ineffective, inefficient and fragmented way.

iv)   Motivational people processes

The fourth key element of success is ensuring that people throughout the firm are highly motivated; without high levels of motivation no firm will perform at the level required to remain competitive. Achieving and maintaining high levels of motivation requires attention to every aspect of people management from recruitment, training and development through coaching, mentoring and performance evaluation and feedback. This needs to occur in an environment where there is clarity concerning performance expectations with such performance expectations derived directly from the firm's strategic objectives taking into account market expectations; and while people are supported to achieve these levels there can be no long-term tolerance of persistent underperformance.

A complementary aspect of a motivational approach to people management is there being a clear career progression open to all with both transparency and equal opportunity being seen to operate at all times and in a fair way.

v)   Powerful client relationships

The fifth element of success is strong and enduring client relationships with a significant group of clients who consistently require and purchase the 'core package' of services the firm provides. The relationships with such clients are characterised by both depth and breadth and while quite possibly 'anchored' around a small number of individuals on each side (perhaps just one) they are nevertheless essentially 'institutionalised' and could be reasonably expected to 'outlive' the tenure of the current 'guardians' of the relationship. Such relationships tend to be built on genuine in-depth knowledge of clients' businesses, their strategies and objectives, the sector within which they operate and the trends within this, and so on. There needs to be strong commitment to clients' success. And, equally importantly, there has to be mutual trust and respect. Based on this there is a genuine opportunity to create considerable value for clients and this is recognised by clients as occurring on an ongoing basis.

Summary

Achieving all the above is hugely challenging. It requires considerable commitment and resources and while the temptation may be to question whether all this can be achieved and afforded the reality is that it must be achieved and afforded if a firm is to have a realistic chance of establishing a long term and profitable future.

The scale of investment is undoubtedly considerable and this in its own rights drives some firms to consider merger in the hope that it will lead to the economies of scale or simply scale to fund such investment.

Experience indicates, however, that such hopes are largely not fulfilled and that mergers driven primarily by financial considerations of cutting costs or building scale are rarely successful. In the short term such mergers do sometimes, although not always, achieve the cost reductions hoped for but tend to do little to improve fundamental competitiveness and simply result in the bringing together of two (or more) firms which for a period may enjoy certain cost based advantages but these tend to be eroded over time.

In reality the primary and only strategically valid reason for merger between legal practices is to improve competitiveness in pursuit of specific strategic objectives and against the backdrop of the changed and changing nature of the marketplace it is this that we will explore in the next chapter.

2
Strategy and Merger

Clear strategy as a precursor to merger

In the first chapter an overview of the trends in the legal market and the impact of these on levels of competition were explored. The consequences are clear with clients increasingly recognising that differing types of legal work are of differing levels of importance and value to them and that differing capabilities are required from law firms depending on the work type and perceived value focus.

For the most business critical matters experience, innovative technical expertise, critical mass, true commerciality, exceptional service delivery capabilities and reputation tend to be the most important characteristics; while for lower value work price, technical competence and delivery on schedule tend to be the prime capabilities required.

The more enlightened law firms recognised the growing sophistication of clients sometime ago and realised that such developments would force them to make choices. In particular they recognised that clients are able to differentiate between genuine competitiveness and broad competence in undertaking legal work and as part of this saw that while in the past broad competence was sufficient to win work and satisfy clients it would not be in the future. More sophisticated and discerning clients would be increasingly able to distinguish between the two and would select and instruct firms accordingly.

These firms also recognised quickly the impossibility of being competitive in everything. For one thing the economic structure of a firm competing for business critical, high value work would make that firm price-uncompetitive for the lower value, fee sensitive work. The cost structure of a firm competing at the higher value end of the market can be 4 or 5 times the level of a firm competing for low value work. This is in part in terms of salary costs (for both lawyers and support staff) but also in terms of infrastructure costs (premises, IT, library, knowledge management, 24/7 operations, and so on).

But it is not only the differing cost structure required to compete at differing points in the market that causes difficulties. It is also in matters such as the leverage (the ratio of equity partners to other fee earners), that tends to be lower in firms doing higher value work because the complexity of such work requires greater partner input, the working procedures – largely bespoke in higher value work and largely standardised around lower value work, the behavioural norms and expectations – excellence in everything around higher value work, more to predefined, specified protocols for lower value work, and so on.

Hence, these more forward looking and strategically-minded firms made choices in terms of the client types they would serve, the work types they would offer and the value positioning they would focus on and built their capabilities accordingly.

These firms become recognised in the market as providing superior services that better met clients' needs and expectations than the firms that were not developing such capabilities and this in turn led to even higher levels of discrimination by buyers of legal services. Thus the fundamental principles of competition accelerated the process of 'winners' and 'losers' emerging in each jurisdiction, in each part of each market and in each major practice area with the 'winners' having the opportunity to create a self-reinforcing cycle that supports the maintenance of their position of leadership: best clients, best instructions, best people, best margins, best supporting infrastructure, best service, best clients and so on. Meantime, other firms – those competent in an area but unable to match the levels of performance of the winners – become squeezed into a lower and often less attractive market position and, as indicated previously are likely to slip into a self-reinforcing downward cycle.

The implications of these factors are clear and in all legal markets there is a recognition that strategy is no longer an interesting business school concept but a genuine sine qua non in terms of future survival, development and prosperity. The outlook for those firms that are broadly competent, but lack genuine competitiveness is clearly increasingly unattractive and this is increasingly recognised. Within the major markets it is possible today to see three broad groupings of firms in terms of their strategic development:

- First, there are those that are clear about their strategy and the implications of this. There are high levels of commitment to the strategy within the firm and the strategy is being actively implemented. In some such firms the strategy has been developed through an essentially 'natural' process of evolution with no apparent structured process leading to its existence but its existence and commitment to it are strong. In other firms similar outcomes have been achieved but by following a more formal or structured process to strategy development (which may or may not have involved external assistance).

- The second group of firms has achieved some success in defining their strategy but for one reason or another has made little progress in actually implementing the strategy; this may be because the implications of the strategy have not really been identified or because while there is conceptual commitment to a strategy there is more limited commitment to its actual implementation; this can often be the case where the implementation requires significant changes in the behaviour or priorities of partners.

- The third group of firms has essentially made little if any progress in defining a strategy. Such firms tend to operate more as a 'collective' of individual practices or partners than as an organisation with each working more or less independently in pursuit of clients and work. Clearly if the individual practices or partners are particularly able then they will prosper and can be extremely successful but clearly such a model is unlikely to be seen as competitive where a broader, integrated approach requiring a number of multiple specialisms is needed and the long-term ability of such firms to attract and retain both the most able lawyers and most attractive clients is limited. In some such firms internal competitiveness can also be prevalent, hampering the ability of partners to cooperate effectively with each other.

Of course widespread commitment to a strategy is no guarantee of success – the strategy may be invalid or flawed; alternatively other firms may have developed and be implementing better strategies or the same strategy better. There is also the possibility that changing clients' needs and expectations and/or the activities of competitors may make the strategy redundant.

None of these factors however constitutes a valid reason for not developing a strategy and within a law firm strategy there should be a clear definition, inter alia, of four key components:

- core client base;
- core service range;
- value positioning;
- basis of competitiveness.

Internally, firms need to be structured so that the strategy can be effectively and efficiently executed and in this respect it is vital that the behaviour and priority of all lawyers, and partners in particular, is focused primarily – and in an ideal world exclusively – on the achievement of the strategy.

Achievement of strategy may require a major shift in a firm from its current position or it may be that the strategy requires less dramatic change. Clearly the more ambitious the strategy – relative to the firm's current position – the greater the likelihood that significant change will be required and the more likely there will be a potential role or even need for merger; if the strategy is less ambitious – relative to the firm's current position – there is a greater likelihood that it can be achieved without merger although, of course, this does not completely preclude the possibility of merger. Some examples perhaps best illustrate the rationale for mergers to be considered:

i)   A single location major Corporate & Finance practice primarily providing 'transactions' focused services to larger corporate clients and investment banks might have little option but to merge if there was clear evidence that it was losing clients/instructions to competitors with competitive capabilities in a number of jurisdictions and it was clear that building comparable capabilities needed to be achieved more rapidly than might be achieved through developing overseas offices on a 'green-field' basis.

ii) Similarly, an Employment practice, seeking to provide services to clients on a national or international basis may conclude that merger is the only means of achieving the geographical coverage required with the appropriate critical mass in each location within a short time period; building such capabilities organically may take too long and be too expensive and in addition it may be concluded that there is a relatively high likelihood that the critical mass required will not be achieved.

iii) A firm slipping out of the leading group of firms in a location through historically failing to develop or implement an appropriate strategy might conclude that it wished to re-establish itself as one of the leaders. In parallel it might recognise that the ground it had lost on the current leaders – in terms of its client base, its overall capabilities and its ability to bring in higher value work – is of a magnitude that cannot be closed without merger. Hence merger becomes a necessity – either with one of the current leaders or with a firm that has complementary capabilities of a nature that would allow the combined firm to develop capabilities that would position it among the leaders.

iv) A firm recognising that it did not have critical mass in certain key practice areas, relative to the perceived leaders, and was increasingly finding itself not considered for certain types of work and/or by certain clients (both within the agreed strategic focus) because of perceptions concerning its capabilities might conclude that the required increase in scale could not be achieved quickly enough organically or through bolt-ons and that a merger was required.

v) Changes in clients' needs might also necessitate merger. With regard to real estate, for example, a focused Real Estate firm might find itself being squeezed out of higher value work because of an absence of, say, corporate, tax, planning, construction, structured financing or environmental capability that are increasingly perceived as critical capabilities around higher value real estate development and investment work. Such a firm might for any number of reasons be unable to develop such capabilities organically or through lateral hiring and hence conclude it needed to merge.

vi) A firm with a clear strategy may face particular challenges regarding its future leadership: there may be nobody suitable or capable or willing to take over the role or there may be too many of the existing partners all reaching retirement at broadly the same time. While unusual, such circumstances do occur particularly in smaller practices and can constitute a valid reason to consider merger.

vii) A final example concerns a firm needing to be of a significantly larger scale in order to have the resources to invest in technology to remain competitive in terms of say 'unit' costs, service delivery and quality. In areas such as claimant personal injury, lower value property matters or volume insurance defence work there are increasing demands for efficiency and maintaining very tight control over costs that necessitate heavy investment in technology. Such investment might only be feasible economically in a firm of a certain size and hence a firm of a substantially smaller size may conclude that it has to merge in order to have the scale to afford the investment required to remain competitive. Without the scale it cannot invest in technology, will become increasingly uncompetitive and, over time, lose its client base to more price competitive competitor firms.

In each of the above examples there are three common factors:

- each firm understands its current position and has a clear idea of where it is trying to get to (or the market position it wishes to maintain);
- each has identified the nature and scale of the 'gap' between where it currently is and where it wishes to be;
- each recognises that merger is either the only or certainly the best way of bridging this gap.

In each example merger is a means to achieve a specific strategy and is not, as frequently seems to be the case, perceived as a strategy in its own right: merger is a means to an end *not* an end in itself. The starting point with each is a clearly articulated, valid strategy with merger identified as a means or a necessity to realise this and it is a better (or the only) way of achieving this in comparison to any other option.

In this context it is important to recognise that client perception may play a very major role. A firm may, for example, be as capable of serving a particular group of clients as any of its competitors. Those competitors may, however, have a perceived advantage through, say, a broader practice capability, a greater number of lawyers or more extensive office network. In practice, such attributes may be quite immaterial in terms of the quality and competitiveness of the service provided; in fact on an objective analysis they could even be found to detract from the quality of service provided. Nevertheless, clients may perceive, or have been persuaded to perceive by competitor firms that larger, broader capabilities are a competitive advantage even though in reality they have no or very limited impact on the quality of service provided. The smaller more focused firm might attempt to convince clients and prospective clients of the flaw in the prevailing reasoning but meet limited success in this respect. In such circumstances there clearly is an argument that there is a valid rationale to merge even though it results in little if any tangible improvement in the service or value delivered. Thus issues of perception can in certain circumstances constitute a valid reason for merger even if such merger results in little if any tangible difference in the service provided or value delivered.

In this context, it is worth pointing out that there are circumstances where merger may be appropriate but it is not directed at helping a firm achieve its current strategy. This is where a firm with an existing strategy is approached by a second firm with a proposal to merge and achieve certain objectives that are outside the approached firm's current strategy but that on evaluation constitute a more attractive option than the strategy currently being pursued.

An example perhaps best illustrates this. A small Corporate practice focused on, say, M&A could have a strategy based around providing such services to small and mid-market corporate clients. If, however, it was approached by, say, a larger Corporate practice in the same city or a larger Corporate practice based in a different city or jurisdiction, this might offer it the opportunity to continue to focus where its strengths and interests lay but in addition ensure that its better clients did not outgrow it as they grew larger. It might also allow the approached firm to provide services to the approaching firm's client base – say to provide services to the corporate clients of the firm from outside the region. The firm might also conclude that such a merger might help it retain and motivate its most ambitious partners who were keen to undertake more demanding work. In such circumstances the Corporate boutique might conclude that it wished to pursue the merger and in effect adopt the strategy of the firm that had approached it because it found that strategy more attractive than the strategy it had been pursuing to that point.

Underlying any consideration of merger there needs to be a recognition that merger on its own will almost always not accomplish much per se and, as an example, putting two mid-size firms together really only creates a larger mid-size firm. Greater scale, increased breadth and depth of capability and an enlarged client base may create opportunities but will not, without significant effort and commitment, lead to greater competitiveness nor will it automatically address or eradicate problems or shortcomings present in firms prior to merger. This is a point explored in greater depth in Parts II and III but at this point it is important that this is recognised: in the same context that merger needs to be recognised as a means to an end and not an end in itself, it is important to recognise that merger can provide a platform to improve competitiveness and achieve strategic objectives but it will deliver neither without significant partner and management effort and focus.

It follows from the above that while there exist many, many invalid reasons to merge there is essentially only one valid reason, namely as the best means to achieve a specific and agreed strategy which leads to a position of improved competitiveness.

Within this context merger can be primarily for offensive or defensive reasons or possibly some combination of the two.

Offensive mergers

The essentially offensive reasons for merger are concerned with achieving a particular identified market position. In such circumstances merger is concerned with assisting a firm make a transformation from its current position to an alternative one that has been identified that requires it to achieve some form of shift in its client base and/or its service offering and/or its value positioning and/or on the basis upon which it competes. Examples of each follow:

- a client base shift could involve, for example, focusing increasingly on listed corporates compared to previously acting largely for owner managed and privately controlled clients;
- a service-offering shift could involve offering a broader range of services to clients; for example providing transactional as well as non-transactional commercial services to clients; or alternatively contentious as well as non-contentious services;
- a shift in value positioning could involve increasing the percentage of higher value instructions won from existing clients; for example being perceived as capable of undertaking large high value real estate portfolio transactions when previously the focus had been on single premises transactions;
- a shift in the basis of competing might occur where changes in clients' expectations have occurred – for example, clients increasingly regarding price as a key determinant of competitiveness or alternatively its advisers having a broader geographic coverage. In either case merger might be the best or only way to achieve such competitive capabilities.

Frequently, of course, there may be a shift on several or even all of these dimensions although this would, prima facie, indicate a relatively more substantial 'gap' between a firm's current position and that to which it aspires and in general terms this is likely to necessitate more widespread and radical changes along with all the risks and challenges associated with this.

An offensive merger might involve merging with a firm already close to the market position desired or alternatively merging with a firm also some distance from the desired position but with shared objectives and analysis having indicated that the two firms combined have the potential as a single entity to achieve that position. For example, a strong pensions practice and a strong employment practice combining to develop as a strong HR firm or two or more regionally focused insurance defence firms combining to provide national coverage to insurance companies. The underlying objective on any offensive merger is to be able to attract and service clients and work that could not be attracted and serviced without merger.

Defensive mergers

Defensive reasons for merger are essentially concerned with maintaining an existing market position or strengthening competitiveness within such a position. Defensive merger could be appropriate for a number of reasons but in particular:

i) Changing client expectations and needs that require a firm to develop new capabilities to be considered competitive for certain types of work; this might for example include a greater breadth of services or depth of expertise, broader geographic coverage, and so on.

ii) Competitor firms' growth might make a firm have, or be perceived to have, inadequate strength-in-depth. As explained earlier this might be merely a perception but increasingly it appears that there are broad similarities in critical mass (by practice area) of the leading firms in any sector. Put another way, it is relatively unusual to find leading firms in a practice area or market sector that are very significantly smaller than their peer group. There may, of course, be non-leading firms of a similar or even greater critical mass but that is a different point and sometimes, but not always, a consequence of firms not distinguishing between size and capability.

For example, currently in the London market, a firm wishing to be seen as competitive in one hundred million pound plus transactions is likely to require c.75 plus Corporate and associated lawyers and a leading Real Estate practice in the same market is likely to have to be of a broadly similar size. Hence, a second defensive reason for merger is to maintain critical mass although care needs to be exercised here to ensure that the greater size does indeed lead to greater critical mass and improved competitiveness and not simply more lawyers.

iii) A third and more extreme defensive reason for merger is as a means to address a crisis such as: the defection of a number of key partners or clients; imminent financial collapse; a significant challenge to a firm's integrity or professionalism; a major difference in opinion over a firm's future direction but with none of the disagreeing 'factions' having the capabilities or option to strike out independently. In such circumstances merger is more often primarily concerned with salvaging what can be saved and/or very rapidly stabilising a potentially catastrophic situation; furthermore time considerations can often have to take precedence over strategic considerations and finding an acceptable resolution immediately may be critical rather than holding out for a strategically more valid merger for some point in the future – the firm's position may be such that it simply doesn't have the luxury of such time.

Mergers brought about by crisis are almost always highly emotional and also almost always have to be completed under extreme time pressure. A structured analytical approach is often not feasible in such circumstances – *'who might we merge with now?'* often becomes the driver rather than considerations of strategic rationale. Nevertheless, the key aspects of the principles and frameworks outlined remain both applicable and valid and the greater the focus that can be given to the issues of strategic direction and business rationale, the more likely the outcome will be positive.

Merger considerations

Irrespective of whether a merger is being considered for offensive or defensive reasons or some combination of the two, there are three sets of issues that need to be considered carefully before embarking down the merger route and these concern:

i)   whether merger is the best way of achieving the strategy;
ii) whether a firm is at a point in its development where it is ready to merge;
iii) the likely reaction of existing core clients to a merger.

These issues are addressed in the following paragraphs.

Merger as the best way to achieve a strategy

While undoubtedly good mergers can assist firms in a major way to achieve their strategic aims they are also, undoubtedly, accompanied by major challenges. Proper analysis and effective planning can certainly help prepare both sides in terms of awareness of these

challenges and this helps in terms of there being realistic expectations of the post-merger implications. Nevertheless, bringing
together two partnerships each with their own history, management,
values, culture, modus operandi, and so on and creating a new firm
and partnership with genuinely enhanced competitiveness is a huge
task even with relatively small firms as parties to the merger.

Integration and achieving the expected benefits of merger requires
huge commitment, dedication and significant resources – both
financial and other. Such benefits do not (unfortunately) emerge
through some process of osmosis but need widespread partner
support and wholesale management attention to be realised.

In parallel, there is likely to be significant disruption as people
'bed down' into a new organisation and structure, 'power-plays' get
worked through and new processes and procedures are introduced.
On top of this there will almost inevitably be personality clashes
and tensions and the potential disruption of resignations as some
partners decide that, after all, the enlarged merged practice is not to
their liking or consider (or are persuaded) that better opportunities
exist elsewhere.

The challenges of achieving post merger integration are discussed
more fully in Part III but at the outset of considering merger as a
means of achieving certain strategic objectives, it is important that
there is a realistic understanding of the challenges of merger and
that these are taken into consideration in deciding whether merger
does represent the most effective way of achieving a strategy.

Clearly in this context if merger is essential – quite literally the
only way of achieving a strategy – then addressing the post-merger
challenges has to be accepted and the major reason for identifying
the main post-merger integration issues is to ensure realistic expectations of the challenges ahead are understood and for planning and
management purposes. (Although it is of course possible that if the
challenges are so great a firm may decide to modify its strategy to
avoid having to address such issues).

If, on the other hand, merger is not the only way of achieving a
strategy, then a focus on both the benefits and challenges that
merger might bring is important in order that an objective, properly
informed decision on whether to proceed with merger is reached.

As a general rule here, the more necessary/essential a merger is to
achieve a strategy the more unavoidable it is to accept the 'down-

sides' that will accompany merger while the less critical merger is to achieving a strategy the more important it is to assess the relative advantages (taking into account both the benefits and challenges) of merger compared to other means of achieving the same outcome. Either way, however, as outlined earlier it is important that these challenges are identified as fully as possible, analysed and discussed so that there is a realistic understanding of them and expectations are kept in line with the likely outcome.

Whether a firm is ready to merge

The second key issue to consider is whether a firm is at a point in its development where it would be able to cope effectively with a merger. It might be, for example, that a firm has a strategically valid rationale to merger but that many of its key partners have not reached a point where they are prepared to become part of a larger firm and potentially lose some of the autonomy and influence they enjoy in a smaller firm.

Assessing whether a firm is at a point where it can not only cope with but also manage to exploit the potential benefits of merger is difficult and there are certainly no straightforward approaches to apply that will work in all circumstances.

To make any such assessment even more difficult, there is an element of testing of 'organisational maturity' here; concerns over the difficulties of reaching a conclusion that the firm is not sufficiently mature at that particular point to deal with merger are significant.

Despite testing of a firm's ability to deal with merger being very difficult, there are a number of areas that can and should be explored and these can provide useful indicators. One such area is the extent to which people genuinely work together providing services to clients and a useful indicator to consider here concerns the levels of cross-selling and working in teams. A low level of cross-selling and working in teams when there exists evidence that clients do require a broad range of legal services could be for a number of reasons, but one in particular to explore is whether this is because of the way partners work and therefore, an indicator of a 'my client' culture. If this is widespread it is one indicator that the firm might not yet be ready for merger.

A second area to focus on concerns attitudes towards, and the role of, management. As firms become larger there tends to need to be a more structured approach to management in order to ensure that the firm operates effectively and efficiently and that the various parts are appropriately integrated. In a smaller firm and also in firms that are less mature in their development there tends to be a less formal or structured approach to management and a lower level of appreciation of its role. There are, of course, exceptions here and indeed some very mature firms manage to maintain a highly informal and unstructured approach to management. Nevertheless, within any firm where there remains high levels of questioning of the principles of requiring a formal management structure and processes, there are likely to be issues about its readiness to cope with merger, particularly if the firm created by merger is likely to require a more structured approach to management in order to operate effectively.

A third area to explore is whether sufficient discussion and debate has occurred so that people are properly aware of the potential implications of merger. It is quite common to find people comfortable with the broad concept of merger but extraordinarily naïve concerning what this might mean in practice, in other words, being part of a larger firm i.e. potentially having to change their working approach, being a part of a more structured organisation, greater accountability and so on. Such discussion may identify an underlying sentiment held by some or many partners which is essentially: *'I don't mind merging as long as it has no impact on me personally'*. There is a clear issue here if a substantial numbers of partners feel like this as an inevitable impact of merger on people is that it does require behavioural change if the benefits identified are to be realised.

Such investigations may reveal that a firm is not yet at a point in its development where it should consider merger. Alternatively it may become clear that more internal discussion is required as an intervening or parallel process in order that there is a strong level of awareness of the likely implications of merger. Omitting to do this is risky since it is likely to become apparent in merger discussions that levels of awareness of the implications of merger are not properly understood and this will likely impact adversely on the outcome.

Reaction of clients to merger

The third area to explore concerns existing key clients' likely reaction to a possible merger and the implications of this on their future instruction of the firm. This is not to suggest that a detailed due diligence exercise should necessarily be undertaken at this stage and in many sets of circumstances, for a range of reasons, it may be quite inappropriate to even mention to clients that merger is being considered.

On the other hand, there may be circumstances where it is entirely appropriate to bring major clients into the thinking at an early stage and, of course there are circumstances where it is the major clients themselves that are 'pushing' a law firm towards merger. In most cases, however, it is entirely possible to take soundings from clients and while clients are likely to recognise the reasons that this is occurring there is no reason for this to lead to such thinking moving into the public domain; besides clients are likely to be pleased that their views are valued and being sought. Such discussions are probably best focused around just a small group of the most significant clients – in many firms the top 10 or so clients account for c.20% or more of total fee income. In most circumstances such clients will have as their principal point of contact in the law firm different partners and hence no single partner would be hugely burdened in terms of the time commitment to take such soundings (over a lunch or drink is often appropriate). While by no means necessarily the case, a firm's most significant clients are more likely to be broadly satisfied with the services being provided – otherwise why are they instructing the firm so extensively? Hence, a discussion focused on the future needs and expectations of such clients and whether the firm might be better able to meet them if it were to be part of a larger organisation is likely to be fruitful. (If in the unlikely event the client is not currently satisfied with the services being provided then at least the firm will achieve vital information about this through the sort of discussion suggested and will thus be in an informed position to take corrective action).

Obviously a key issue to explore in discussions is whether merger might in any way adversely impact on clients' perceptions of or level of instructions to the firm. In response to such issues there is likely to be a degree of caution and caveats concerning who the firm might merge with and their market profile, reputation and capability and so on; nevertheless, useful information can almost always be obtained. Such meetings can also provide an opportunity to assess in a preliminary way attitudes towards 'business conflict' in terms of how clients would feel if, as a consequence of merger, competitors of theirs or other clients in the same market sector were to be clients of the enlarged firm. It is important to stress that this is concerned with business as opposed to legal conflict.

There might also be some discussion (where appropriate) concerning whether a broader geographic coverage might lead to the firm being better able to meet client expectations or whether clients see little benefit in having the firm being able to service them more widely and/or they are currently highly satisfied with the services competitor firms are providing in other locations.

If these discussions indicate that a number of core clients are actually opposed to the firm merging or see it offering little, if any, benefit to them these are clearly important issues to bring into the next stages of the decision making. On the other hand, if such clients are supportive of or neutral towards the possibility of merger, useful input can often be gained in terms of the characteristics and capabilities that should be sought in a potential merger partner.

The role of alliances

An important consideration is whether an alliance on joint venture might provide a better or as good a means of achieving the strategic objectives or might play a useful role as a 'stepping stone' on the route to full merger.

Alliances and joint ventures can play a useful role in certain circumstances but it is important to be aware from the outset of certain significant shortcomings inherent in such approaches. For obvious reasons alliances historically have primarily been seen and used as a route forward when firms are seeking to broaden their geographic capabilities. The first potential shortcoming is that from a client perspective alliances can rarely guarantee the level of consistency that can be delivered by a single firm and in particular there is not the same 'vested' authority in client partners to ensure that high levels of service are indeed provided from all offices.

At this point (2005) it would be wrong to suggest that firms who have merged internationally are uniformly performing perfectly in these respects and client feedback shows that this is clearly not the case. On the other hand, clients do recognise the improvements being achieved by many international firms in terms of consistency: clients also recognise that the more successful merged firms are making strong progress in instilling the concept of 'a core client anywhere, a core client everywhere' and core client partners are being seen as having the authority to 'command' resources wherever they are required.

Hence if a key objective is to ensure consistency across a number of jurisdictions then neither alliances nor joint ventures are likely to provide a long-term solution.

A second, potentially substantial shortcoming with alliances and joint ventures is that there tends not to be the same level of commitment compared with mergers to making them work. They tend to be seen primarily as providing resource to be used when appropriate and hopefully also a useful source of referral work. There tends not, however, to be sufficient commitment nor priority to address challenges in achieving effective inter-office working except on a matter by matter basis nor the same urgency around joint marketing and the like. Of course there are circumstances where such shortcomings are not of paramount importance and hence alliances and joint ventures represent an appropriate way forward.

In overall terms, however, there is limited evidence with just one or two notable exceptions to indicate that they do represent a viable long term way forward and the successes to date have all involved firms in specific and unusual market positions rather than in the 'mainstream' market. Having made this point this is not to imply that alliances and joint ventures are an absolute 'non-starter' as a first step in a long term approach or for firms with only occasional needs for capabilities outside say their existing geographical scope; however so far there are very few examples of such arrangements working as a directly competitive alternative to merger on a long term basis.

Where there certainly is potentially a valuable role for alliances and joint ventures is as a 'stepping stone' to full merger. For any number of reasons firms may not be able to merge immediately but do see real benefits in moving beyond the sort of relationships typified in a 'best friends' approach or being part of an international network. The reasons for not merging immediately can be varied and could, for example, be driven by significant difference in the firms in values, culture, structure, management, compensation, profitability and so on which cannot be bridged at the present time or alternatively there needs to be some programme – possibly in both firms – of convergence before merger can take place.

In Europe in particular there have been a number of cases where merger has been preceded by a period of alliance and in many of these cases this has been considered as the only option to pursue as a means of ultimately achieving merger.

Part II

Preparing for Merger

3
Whether to Merge and with Whom

The first part of the book set out a number of key issues for firms to consider regarding market trends and their own strategic development and in the context of these to assess the role that merger might play. Two overriding principles for those considering merger have been put forward:

i) merger is a means to an end not an end in itself; its role is to assist and drive a firm from its current market position to a future, preferred position of greater competitiveness;
ii) alternative means of achieving the transformation from the current position to the desired future position are likely to be available; merger should only be considered when it is clearly the best (or only) way of achieving the transformation.

It follows from this that if merger is genuinely essential in order to achieve a strategy then there should be less concern on whether to merge or not and a primary focus on identifying who to merge with – the need for merger is not the issue in these circumstances although there may be issues of timing to consider. On the other hand, if the need to merge is not so strong although merger still represents the best way of achieving a strategy, there should be a greater focus on evaluating the balance of advantages and disadvantages of a merger to ensure that it does represent the best way forward.

There will also be circumstances where merger opportunities emerge although merger is not considered a priority by a firm as the best way for it to achieve its strategy. In these circumstances, the merger opportunity may well be worth exploring but it is unlikely that it would be pursued except if the advantages it offered were felt to be considerable and the disadvantages minimal.

Before exploring the process of establishing whether or not to merge, it is worth reviewing three sets of circumstances where a number of mergers have taken place and based on the principles outlined above, there is not a strong rationale.

Size for size sake

A number of mergers have led to firms increasing in size, sometimes considerably. Such mergers have been driven by a variety of factors, some valid (concerned with improving competitiveness) but many others invalid. Among the less valid reasons have been:

- to be the largest firm in a city, region or country;
- to maintain a certain size relative to the largest firms;
- vanity/ego based growth.

In most markets, at both a national and local level, it is relatively easy to identify such firms. They tend to be among the largest (and often make a considerable play on their size) but are not considered among the leaders in terms of practice skills or market sector excellence, tend to have a more variable quality of partner, operate in a relatively heterogeneous way with relatively low levels of consistency, achieve relatively lower fees per fee earner and have profit per partner some way below that of the leading firms. Interestingly, the increase in size of these firms may well have raised clients' expectations of the level of service they will receive yet the combined firm is delivering no higher quality of service than its predecessor parts, contributing to client dissatisfaction because the gap between client expectations and perceived service received has widened.

Building an extensive office network

A second set of mergers has been largely focused on building extensive networks of offices on a national and/or international basis but there has been no overriding business rationale for such a network and no real strategy behind it: the development of the office network has been neither client driven/demanded nor 'supply' pushed in terms of the firm having some specific highly competitive capabilities in one office that it wishes to exploit further by exporting them to another office and thereby increase the size of the market it can reach.

These multi-office firms that lack a strategic rationale can also often be relatively easily identified and two characteristics in particular tend to stand out:

- the focus of each office's practice mix and client base varies significantly with no apparent priority or commitment to achieving convergence;
- there is little if any mutual dependency between the offices – each is largely a stand-alone operation and could relatively easily operate as effectively outside of the merged firm.

Financially driven mergers

Some initial thinking on law firm merger was driven by an assumption that merger would lead to economies of scale on the support side and/or opportunities to increase fee rates. Although there is some evidence of the very largest law firms achieving certain economies of scale in most cases mergers do not deliver economies of scale and indeed in many cases firms have discovered that merger actually leads to an increase in the cost base rather than any saving. The argument, that has proved to be invalid is that two Accountancy departments, two IT departments, two HR departments and so on could be combined into one and considerable savings be achieved. The first part of the argument may be correct but the second has repeatedly been shown to be largely incorrect with opportunities to make savings through eradicating duplicate positions and functions offset by the need to have higher calibre and hence more costly support personnel.

In addition, larger firms tend to be more complex and require higher levels of management and co-ordination to operate effectively – all of which have cost implications and/or eat into fee earning time. The thinking that larger firms can charge higher rates simply because of their size has equally been shown in practice to be quite fallacious.

In the future there may well be mergers that are largely financially driven and this may be expected, in particular, in the lower value parts of the market where scale may be a means to achieve lower 'unit' costs. In practice, however, it is likely to be the case of firms with the most effective and efficient internal systems, that provide them with a clear cost and service advantage, taking over or absorbing less efficient competitors, stripping out their entire infrastructure and 'plugging' the fee earners into the existing operating infrastructure. While it can be argued that this is a financially driven merger it is in reality merger (or perhaps more accurately take-over) driven by process and critical mass considerations.

Having reviewed three of the more questionable reasons for merger, let us now turn to the process of establishing whether a rationale for merger does exist, and if so, establishing the broad criteria to be sought in a merger partner.

To merge or not

In the vast majority of legal practices the decision to merge requires the support of a significant majority of partners. In a small number of firms, a simple majority may be sufficient but in most firms a two thirds or three quarters level of partner support is required and although now increasingly unusual, there are firms which require unanimity of partner support to proceed with merger: or put a different way, a single vote against can stop a firm proceeding with merger.

This requirement for significant levels of support is obviously important from the point of view of simply achieving a merger but it is, in practice, even more important from the point of view of making a merger work. Partners might for a variety of reasons vote for proceeding with a merger even though they don't really support it: they may feel threatened by the departure of key partners known to be in favour of merger or be agreeing to merger for fear of appearing conservative or non-entrepreneurial otherwise. In such circumstances the absence of genuine support is likely to result in a decreased commitment to making the merger work and clearly if there are a significant number of partners in this camp there is an increased likelihood of the merger not succeeding or certainly not realising its full potential. Hence, for any firm contemplating merger, it is important to achieve widespread and genuine commitment to merger as opposed to lukewarm acquiescence or, at worst, reluctant compliance. This raises important issues in that it necessitates developing high levels of genuine commitment and support for merger across the partnership at some point in the process. At what point this should occur is not a straightforward issue to address.

In some circumstances the commitment will have been developed because a strategy review will have persuaded partners that the only or best way of achieving their strategic ambitions is through merger.

Most cases, however, are less clear cut than this. As outlined in the next chapter in many firms there is a partnership deed or governance requirement for management to have a mandate from the partnership authorising them to enter into initial exploratory discussions. Such a mandate, however, is not the same as having partnership commitment. While in an ideal world it might be argued that having real commitment at the outset is preferred, for practical reasons this is often not possible because it is only as those delegated by the partnership to explore merger options undertake their work can the detailed case for merger be established and commitment developed. Nevertheless within any firm contemplating merger the fundamental case that demonstrates that merger is the only or clearly the best way to achieve the desired strategy needs to be developed and needs to be understood by, and receive high levels of support from, all partners. Obviously, every firm is different in terms of its existing position, its aspirations, the levels of competition it faces, its marketplace, and so on. Hence, for every firm there is a unique set of circumstances to be considered and a specific business case to be developed. In broad terms, however, Figure 3.1 illustrates how the rationale for or against merger needs to go through a number of stages which may be part of a structured process or occur on a more 'informal' basis:

A number of issues need to be considered in reviewing both the current and future position of a firm including:

- market, client and competitor trends;
- work mix;
- client type focus;
- geographic capabilities;

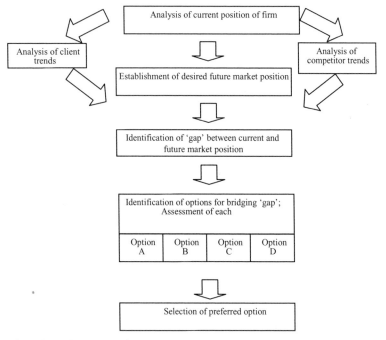

Figure 3.1 Assessment Stages

- reputation and profile;
- competitive capabilities;
- size;
- structure;
- economics;
- internal environment;
- management.

The greater the gap between the current position and that desired, the greater the likelihood of a need for merger although this is only a broad guide and much also depends on a firm's inherent capabilities to affect major change successfully.

Figure 3.2 illustrates seven dimensions along which law firms have typically competed in the market place. It is important in reviewing the firm's position in the market to understand and evaluate the areas in which it currently competes and differentiates itself

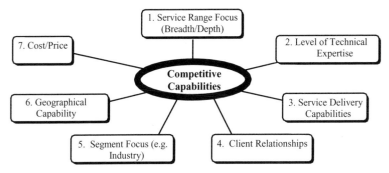

Figure 3.2   Seven Competitive Dimensions

as well as how the merged firm might seek to compete. In recent years, competition has led to firms needing to be highly capable on most if not all of these dimensions with firms increasingly seeking to differentiate themselves on 'higher level dimensions' such as being able to offer a consistent service across jurisdictions, offering a multidisciplinary approach to an industry sector, their levels of commitment to their clients' success, the commerciality of their approach, advice and services and so on.

In Chapter 2 a number of examples of reasons to merge were outlined. In practice there are four valid generic drivers of merger:

1) to develop greater critical mass and hence competitiveness in key practice areas as a means to service existing clients better and/or to attract new clients of the type desired;
2) to develop complementary capabilities in order to offer a broader range of services to protect and/or develop a position with existing clients and/or to attract new clients of the type desired;
3) to expand geographic capabilities in order to 'export' existing practice strengths and/or to service existing clients more extensively and/or to have the capabilities to undertake certain types of work (e.g. international M&A transactions or Capital Markets work);
4) to develop greater market share rapidly in key market sectors; this can often be for work that is fee sensitive with the increased volume providing the opportunity to be able to invest more extensively in systems and technology and thus be more price competitive and/or be able to offer a more responsive service.

In each of the above cases merger is part of a process of improving competitiveness and while the merger by itself will likely achieve limited impact in itself, it provides the platform to achieve specific strategic objectives.

There are a small number of other valid reasons for merger but these tend to be a reflection of very particular circumstances. Examples include:

1) to reduce exposure to a very cyclical market sector, client or type of work;
2) to bring in new leadership/management and/or a more sophisticated supporting infrastructure;
3) to address an impending crisis such as severe cash flow problems, departure of a significant number of key partners, etc.

It would appear that in the past a considerable number of mergers failed to have a valid strategic rationale or, if they did, the intentions of the merger were never realised. This conclusion is based on the fact that such mergers created bigger firms but not more competitive firms and in practice because clients tend to have higher expectations of larger firms and because larger firms tend to be more complex (and expensive) to manage, the firms created through this type of merger often ended up relatively less competitive rather than more competitive.

In many jurisdictions, including both the US and Europe, examples of merged firms that are large but not particularly competitive or profitable can be identified. There are equally many smaller firms, also created through merger, that are no more competitive than prior to merger although because of their size they tend to be less in the spotlight. The outlook for these firms tends to be unpromising and such firms should act as a useful warning to those contemplating merger.

For merger to be successful there has to be a strong strategic underpinning and there has to be a genuine understanding of and commitment to making the necessary changes to ensure that merger does deliver the benefits identified.

There is significant benefit in producing a paper, based on objective analysis, of the strategic rationale for merger for consideration by a partnership: the discipline of producing this is highly worthwhile and its exposure to critical examination by partners tends to be invaluable. Furthermore it brings all partners into the process and in this respect provides a useful opportunity to begin building commitment.

Establishing the required capabilities for a merger partner

Having concluded that merger is an appropriate option to pursue, the next issue to confront is to determine with whom. In some circumstances it may be appropriate to address such an issue in a largely intuitive or instinctive way; in the main however, it is far preferable to follow a more structured approach based on:

- developing a clear profile of the characteristics, both tangible and intangible, sought in a merger partner;
- identifying a list of potential partners who, prima facie, appear to match such characteristics.

Throughout this process a balance of realism and pragmatism must be maintained. It is more than likely that the ideal or 'perfect' match to the profile developed doesn't exist: or maybe exists but for one reason or another is not interested in merger. For example, the profile of the merger partner may dictate that a leading reputation and track record in a particular specialism is required but initial research shows that none of the leading firms in this specialism are interested in merger. The issue that then has to be addressed is whether a non-leading practice, if, say, it had an up-and-coming reputation, might be acceptable and the answer to this question might well be dependent on whether such a firm had partners with the ability, ambition and commitment to develop the top tier ranking identified as required.

Developing a profile of the type of merger partner sought is best done in a structured way and the table in Figure 3.3 provides a useful framework for defining the capabilities and characteristics required.

A key benefit of completing a table such as this (perhaps taking a page to explore each capability/characteristic) is the focus it provides in establishing the degree to which similar versus complementary characteristics and capabilities are required. A predominance of

Capabilities/Characteristics	Preferred	Acceptable	Importance
Core practice capabilities Size Geographic location Management style Partnership structure Profitability Compensation approach Client base Reputation Other			

Figure 3.3   Framework for Defining Capabilities & Characteristics of Merger Partner

similar characteristics and capabilities to those in existence in the firm seeking merger would indicate a primary aim of building strength in practice areas where the firm already focuses; a predominance of complementary characteristics and capabilities would indicate that an aim of the merger is to achieve a shift or broadening in the focus of the firm.

In addition to developing a profile based on what might reasonably be described as the more tangible or objective characteristics and capabilities there is also a need to consider the 'softer', more intangible and subjective characteristics and capabilities. Such factors are frequently and, in our view, inappropriately lumped together in the catch-all phrase 'culture'.

Law firms do have distinctive cultures but frequently in this context 'culture' is a euphemism – incorrectly – for chemistry i.e. how people get on with one another. Culture is a critical area that needs to be considered. Hence, a profile of the preferred merger partner should also focus on factors such as:

- the role of partners and how they spend their time:
  - hours committed
  - chargeable hours expected and variations
  - focus on practising law compared to delegating/managing others
  - focus on business development and marketing;
- the style of working; largely individualistic or more team based;

- the role of management; primarily supportive and facilitating or more performance management oriented;
- the role of the support departments; considered as peers or primarily service providers;
- the underlying values and behavioural norms.

Again comparing the preferred profile of the ideal merger partner with the current profile of the firm seeking merger will reveal the extent to which reinforcement of the existing status quo is required versus the desire to introduce complementary behavioural norms with merger seen as a means of shifting the culture and modus operandi in the firm seeking merger.

Such analysis can often identify interesting contradictions that need to be resolved; for example, to seek a merger partner with a more active commitment to new business development yet there is a sense within the firm that more 'traditional' values that somewhat denigrate marketing, need to be maintained.

A key factor in drawing up such a profile is to consider the characteristics and capabilities that are of prime importance compared to those that are less crucial so that those responsible for identifying potential firms and conducting initial evaluations have a clear profile and assessment criteria to work to. In many circumstances it is appropriate for this profile to be discussed and approved by the partnership. In part, this is a key aspect of keeping all partners on board and committed to the merger process but it also provides a valuable reference point for later in the process when the acceptability of shortlisted firms is being evaluated.

On this point it is important to recognise that those involved in working on a merger can rapidly become deeply engrossed in the process and spend considerable time thinking about the issues. Those partners outside this group can easily, albeit inadvertently, lose touch with what is occurring (to the extent sometimes of even forgetting – albeit only temporarily – the rationale for considering merger) and while issues of confidentiality and practicality may prevent progress reports and partnership meetings from occurring with great regularity, it is important to keep all partners on board (this point is discussed further in the following chapter) and as part of this process there tends to be a need to review periodically and re-communicate the rationale for merger.

Identifying potential merger candidates

Based on the profile developed describing the characteristics and
capabilities of a preferred merger partner, a search process can
begin.

It is possible that this will be undertaken entirely without external
assistance relying largely on the knowledge of partners backed up by
reference to legal directories, other publications and the like. In
some circumstances such an approach is quite suitable, particularly
when seeking to build strength in depth in a particular geographic
location where all the potential merger partners are known. There
are however certain potential risks in not involving some external
input to the process:

(i)   subjective, and often non-representative anecdotal evidence,
      experience and prejudice of partners (that may also be out of
      date) can drive the process sometimes resulting in very strong
      potential candidates being excluded from inclusion on a
      shortlist;
(ii) shortlists that are assembled internally tend to lack more cre-
      ative or lateral thinking in terms of potential candidates; experi-
      ence indicates that partners in law firms tend not to know the
      market as well as they believe and also tend to view other law
      firms strongly from the perspective of being a competitor rather
      than from a market/client perspective;
(iii) bringing external input to the process of identifying poten-
      tial merger candidates provides a useful opportunity to test
      independently:

      • the rationale that led to merger being considered the most
        effective way of achieving particular strategic objectives;
      • the overall validity of the firm having such objectives;
      • the profile, in terms of characteristics and capabilities, of the
        preferred merger candidate and, indeed, the validity and level
        of realism in these.

At the very least, therefore, it is worthwhile taking the opportunity
of getting some form of external vetting of or soundings on the
firms on a shortlist – if only to check that those firms that are on the

list are justifiably there and that the rationale for those excluded is also sound.

In other circumstances external assistance is an essential element of developing a shortlist. Typically the reasons for seeking external expertise include:

(i) bringing in additional knowledge and/or expertise – this is often the case when a firm is seeking to merge with a practice in a relatively unfamiliar geographic market but this is by no means the only circumstance when such knowledge and expertise is of value;

(ii) bringing independence and objectivity to the process, combined with up-to-date market knowledge. In particular this can help ensure that the process is genuinely driven from the perspective of the overall interests of the firm and thus avoid the risk of the process being 'influenced by parochial interests' or seen to be;

(iii) bringing additional and skilled resources to the process. Carrying out research to identify potential merger candidates and then objectively analyse and evaluate their 'fit' with the agreed profile is a time consuming process. Certainly on larger national and international mergers the process of identifying and then analysing/evaluating candidate firms can require significant time to complete;

(iv) maintaining confidentiality can also be an issue in some circumstances. This is particularly likely to be the case if the process of shortlisting requires the collection of sensitive information from the market concerning, for example, the strength of potential candidate firms' relationships with key clients, gauging candidate firms' likely level of interest in merger, and so on. Again this can more easily, and sometimes only be achieved by utilising external resources.

There are a number of options in terms of where to turn for external advice including merger brokers, headhunters/recruitment agencies, accountants and management consultancies. Ultimately, chemistry will play an important role in selecting external advisers – in an area as sensitive and sometimes as emotional as merger it is difficult to conceive of a positive result emerging when the relationship with the external adviser is not good.

Key issues to address in considering using external advisers to assist with developing a shortlist include:

- the experience of advisers;
- their track record;
- the basis on which they work;
- the basis on which they charge;
- their estimated fees.

Some advisers on merger act very much in a brokerage capacity, essentially matchmaking and offering little if anything beyond the initial introduction. This, of course, may be all that is required and hence represents the best option.

Some firms of accountants who work in this area have a reputation, not in all cases fairly, in only or largely shortlisting firms that are already their existing clients.

Neither of these approaches is necessarily a reason not to appoint such advisers although there are clearly circumstances when neither would be appropriate.

An important consideration in appointing external advisers to assist with the shortlisting process is to consider their suitability for providing assistance later on in the merger process. If it is felt likely that external assistance will also be required in developing a detailed business case, evaluating the pros and cons of a particular merger, in the actual merger discussions themselves, and so on then this may be a factor to take into account when selecting advisers to assist with the shortlisting as there can be distinct advantages in developing a relationship with a single external adviser who can provide support throughout the process.

On this issue it is worthwhile making an important point on fees for external advisers. Some charge on an hourly rate or on a fixed fee basis to undertake a particular, defined piece of work; with such arrangements there is no obvious incentive for advisers to be anything but wholly objective in their advice. Other advisers work largely or wholly on a 'success fee' basis of charging. This can be very attractive from the perspective of there being no fees payable in the event of merger not occurring. The primary drawbacks with such an approach are two-fold. First, there is a likelihood that the advice provided will not be wholly objective (or at least a doubt in the minds of some partners on this point may exist); the adviser clearly has a distinct interest in merger occurring. Second, the level of the success fees can be extraordinarily high – particularly if they are related in some way to a percentage of the combined merging firms' total fee income.

Irrespective of whether external support is used, the process of developing and assessing shortlisted firms has both an objective and more subjective element to it with, in most cases, the former being more important in the early stages and the latter being 'super-imposed' at a later stage.

The first stage in the process is to establish a long list of potential firms from the appropriate 'universe' of firms in a particular location. Such a universe may be relatively broadly defined such as: 'all corporate firms in city/region X which are considered to have a leading reputation in practice areas V, W and Y' or all firms with a leading practice in Z in any of the primary or secondary cities in a region or jurisdiction. Alternatively, the universe may be very specifically defined in terms of size of firm, reputation, and so on.

In some circumstances the definition of the universe can require a degree of interpretation; say 'any firm that can assist us achieve our objectives of becoming/maintaining a position as a leading firm in practice area X and/or geographic location Y'.

Irrespective of the definition of the universe, initial long-listing tends to rely primarily on a judicious mix of desk research, legal directories, the Internet and the like combined with market knowledge and a degree of creative thinking.

The more objective initial assessment of potential firms will be based on clear criteria covering factors such as, for example, geographic location, practice area strengths, headcount, transactions track record, quality of client base, economic performance, and so on. Based on such criteria; potential firms can be assessed (possibly using a 5-point scale where 5 equates to a very strong/excellent match on each criteria and 0 equates to a very weak/poor match). Adding the individual scores will result in an aggregate score for each firm with those scoring most highly being the initial, most promising, prospects. In some circumstances a more sophisticated approach to the scoring may be appropriate. For example, it may be decided that any candidate firm scoring less than say '4' on a particular criteria might be automatically excluded and/or weightings might be applied to certain criteria to reflect their relative importance. Figure 3.4 illustrates a relatively simple approach to evaluating potential firms.

In the past and still to some extent today, some assessments give very significant weight to comparability of profit per equity partner (PPEP) in developing short lists of potential merger candidates.

It would be wrong to say that this is wholly inappropriate and of course levels of profitability do provide an important indication on factors such as the market reputation of the firm, its client base, the type of work it is undertaking, how the firm is managed, how it is structured and how hard people work.

The issue of differences in profit per partner should not, however, automatically rule out firms from a shortlist and accountants in particular have tended to give very substantial weight to this issue.

If a strong business case for merger is found to exist, significant differences in PPEP can be accommodated, certainly during a transitional period, and it is a serious mistake to allow this issue to take on a too significant prominence in identifying potential merger candidates and undertaking initial assessments.

There are many examples of highly successful mergers between firms that initially had considerable differences in their PPEP.

The type of process outlined above will potentially be somewhat over complex where, say, a merger partner is being sought to strengthen the critical mass of a firm operating in a small city or region and where the number of potential candidates (the universe) is extremely limited. Even in such circumstances, however, experience shows that considerable value is derived from identifying and evaluating potential firms in a structured way if only to confirm (or otherwise) existing perceptions of the relative strengths and weaknesses of firms.

Such an exercise can sometimes demonstrate the clearly superior strengths of a particular firm and thereby help counter the prejudices that too commonly can be allowed to impact on the process of identifying potential merger partners and are typified by statements such as: 'Merge with them over my dead body' (in some circumstances perhaps no bad thing!) or 'I'll never merge with them as long as X is a partner there!'

Having developed an initial list of potential firms and refined and ranked firms from this through an objective assessment process as

Firm	Principal Location	Overall Strategic Fit Low : High (1–5)	Size (No. of Lawyers)	Profit per Equity Partner	Revenue	Geographic Locations (No. of Lawyers)				Practice Compatibility Low : High (1–5)			
						A	B	C	D	A	B	C	D
Firm A													
Firm B													
Firm C													
Firm D													
Firm E													
Firm F													

Figure 3.4 Assessment Grid

outlined above, it then becomes appropriate to introduce a degree of more subjective evaluation focusing on the 'softer' issues.

At this point issues such as assessing in more detail the degree of overlap with each candidate firms' strategic aims can be undertaken. Also it will be appropriate to consider the likely interest of each firm in merger, whether merger would represent takeover or a dilution of control and, if so, whether this is an issue*; the perceived level of similarity in the internal environment, style of management, and so on can also be evaluated.

Clearly such evaluations are based, to an extent, on subjective perceptions and it is on issues such as this that external advisers, with in-depth market knowledge and experience, can be of particular value. In particular their observations are likely to be more objective than, say, those of ex-partners (often regarded as a useful source of information) of any firm being assessed in this way especially if such partners left or were 'asked to leave' the firm in strained circumstances.

Based on such a process a final shortlist of preferred merger candidates can be established. This may contain as few as 1 or 2 names but ideally will probably contain 5–10 names as a manageable maximum.

At this point some form of contact needs to be made with each firm to assess their level of interest in principle in merger and the extent to which there is a potential synergy between the two firms' strategic aims.

If it is important to maintain anonymity at this point, such an approach can be made on a no-name basis by an independent third party. Even if anonymity is not an important factor, it may still be advantageous for an independent third party to make the initial approach and circumstances will dictate what is most appropriate.

---

* On this point it is worth reflecting on the position today of a number of law firms that have undertaken a series of small mergers over the years, concerned that merger with a larger firm might result in a loss or dilution of management control. Unfortunately this policy has resulted in such firms successively merging with small firms of not particularly high quality and this ultimately has diluted the overall quality and reputation of the firm. This may be considered an acceptable trade-off if maintaining management control is considered paramount although the dilution in quality raises serious strategic concerns.

Based on the outcome of such initial discussions a final shortlist of potential merger candidates can be drawn up.

At this point an initial meeting with management or senior representatives of each preferred firm is appropriate and these meetings are a key part of the final stages of the process to identify a single, preferred merger candidate. It is important to stress that these meetings should not in any way be about negotiation but be solely concerned with identifying from the shortlist, the single firm with whom the strongest business case for merger is believed to exist.

Each meeting with one of the shortlisted firms should ideally follow a similar agenda (a proposed outline is included in Appendix I) and a consistent framework should also be used to 'evaluate' each candidate firm (see Appendix II). The style and nature of such a framework will inevitably be dictated by the circumstances but for each firm shortlisted should provide a consistent approach to assessing the benefits, shortcomings and drawbacks of merger. Inevitably, such an assessment framework will have both objective and more subjective elements but mere dislike or lack of empathy with the partners met is, in most circumstances, not a sufficient reason in isolation to reject a firm except if such factors are symptomatic of deeper and more significant differences between the two firms. To make these meetings as productive as possible it is normally a good practice to have an exchange of certain information in advance.

Drafting a firm profile is often the easiest means of achieving this and a template is included in Appendix III. The aim of the profile is not to repeat the material, normally highly flattering, included in a firm's publicity material and on its website but to provide an objective overview of the firm, its history, structure, strategy and financial position with a summary of what it wishes to achieve through merger.

The level of financial information included at this initial point is open to debate but in an era where greater transparency concerning financial performance is increasingly the norm there seems little point in being overly coy.

Agreed information is normally exchanged on the basis of strict confidentiality and solely for the purpose of assessing whether there is a potential business case for merger. Some firms take this on trust while others prefer to have a confidentiality agreement in place.

Throughout this process there will be a need to give careful consideration to the level of communication and appropriate consultation with partners. Much will depend on the circumstances, the relative size of the merger parties, the requirement for confidentiality, the level of authority and freedom to act delegated to management – either formally through the Partnership deed or informally by custom and practice, and so on.

Levels of consultation

In the larger national and international firms, high levels of autonomy tend to be delegated to management and assuming any merger being considered, irrespective of who initiated discussions, is consistent with the firm's agreed strategic objectives, then little if any communication or consultation with partners will be expected. In such firms those in central management but not involved in the discussions will likely be kept informed of progress as may other partners in key practice groups and management positions.

In such firms, when a partnership mandate is needed to complete a merger, a paper will be drafted and endorsed by those in key management positions and although a vote will then take place this will largely be a formality particularly if the proposed merger is relatively small in scale compared to the firm's existing position.

In mid-sized firms a more likely process would be for those in management to report back to the partnership at key points in the process (e.g. development of merger criteria, establishment of shortlist, identification of preferred firm, etc.). Broader based consultation with partners is also likely to be expected and this may be undertaken more effectively in, say, smaller practice group or departmental meetings. Again circumstances and the expectations of partners will determine what approach is most appropriate.

In smaller firms a higher level of partnership involvement and consultation tends to be the norm, sometimes to the extent of a verbal or written report being required at every stage in the process and after every meeting with a potential merger partner. There is nothing inherently wrong in such an approach although inevitably it does place an additional and in some circumstances substantial burden on those who are already under considerable pressure in terms of balancing their existing client and/or management responsibilities with potentially significant involvement in merger discussions.

Clearly the preceding is written from the perspective of a law firm that is taking the initiative in respect of merger. There is, of course, the converse set of circumstances when a law firm is approached to gauge its level of interest in merger.

In the current climate of a relatively high level of merger activity and interest it is unlikely that such an approach will be considered as completely 'out of the blue' as there are very few firms that at some point in the recent past have not had merger on the management or partnership agenda or been subject to some form of approach.

For those firms that have a well developed sense of their own strategic direction there should be little difficulty in assessing whether a merger approach is worth considering although of course there are circumstances when such an approach may result in a firm wishing to reassess and possibly change its strategy because of the opportunities opened up by the possibility of a specific merger approach.

For those firms with a less developed sense of their strategic direction an unexpected outside approach is more difficult to assess. Except if such a firm has an absolute commitment not to merge it is probably worth investing in at least an initial meeting and to do so with an open mind. Before that meeting it is worth investing a certain amount of time considering, if only in outline form, the main issues raised in this and previous chapters so as to be in a better position to assess the approach made in as objective a manner as possible.

One final caveat is worth making: in any such meetings, whether as the instigator or the party receiving the approach, it is important to be on guard for the small number of firms who seem to have no genuine intention of merging but use meetings such as these to try and identify recruitment opportunities and the overall 'state of health' of a firm. Most law firms regard such behaviour as wholly unacceptable but in an increasingly competitive market this form of 'asset hunting' does occur from time to time. Guarding against this is an area where experienced external advisers can be of value.

Issues to be addressed prior to merger

Firms considering merger and following the framework outlined above will have undertaken an objective and rational review of their own position and performance and compared this to where they aspire to be. As part of this process, they will have identified the 'gap' between their current position and where they wish to be; and it is merger that is assessed as the most effective means of bridging this gap.

During this review process it is almost inevitable that some shortcomings in the firm will have been identified. Typically these cover certain issues that merger might be expected to address such as lack of critical mass in certain practice areas, too narrow capabilities, lack of geographic coverage, and so on. There may also be issues that merger will not directly address and in particular those concerning performance or, perhaps more accurately, underperformance.

It is not realistic to assume that merger will directly address such issues. If certain people or certain practice areas are underperforming prior to merger the strong likelihood is that they will continue to underperform post-merger except if there are specific factors brought into play by the merger that will address such shortcomings. There are few examples of such circumstances existing although if underperformance is, say, solely a consequence of a lack of work in one firm or part of a firm then merger with a firm with a surfeit of work might address this issue. Even in such circumstances a degree of caution is advisable. Good individual partners, practice areas and firms do not tend to suffer a long term paucity of work and when they do lose work – say due to the loss of a client for reasons not related to their own performance (e.g. the client being taken over or going out of business) then they tend to have the capability and drive to replace such work.

As a general principle, underperformance and other shortcomings should be addressed prior to merger rather than expect either that the merger itself will address such issues or that the issues will in some way be easier to address post-merger. Worst of all is to assume that such shortcomings can be tolerated in a larger firm, post-merger.

In particular, issues of underperformance of partners, be they quality or productivity related, are best dealt with pre-merger. Pre-merger, they are more likely to be addressed with tolerance and compassion by partners and management who have had long term working relations with and knowledge of the underperforming partners. Post-merger, they are more likely to be addressed in a more clinical, objective fashion with less compassion and by a management who may have little understanding or knowledge of the history and circumstances surrounding the situation.

Failing to deal with such situations can, in fact, even jeopardise merger taking place as any firm is likely to have reservations about merging with another firm with underperforming partners or where underperformance is seen to be tolerated. Furthermore, a merger is put at additional jeopardy if early on in the post-merger period partners are seen to be being dismissed; this is destabilising internally and it is the sort of event that the legal press delights in highlighting – potentially causing knock on problems.

An unwillingness to address underperformance pre-merger tends to be a consequence of an unwillingness to confront difficult and often sensitive, issues but it needs to be recognised how misguided and short-sighted this can be.

Of course, there are circumstances where the issue of performance is resolved by merger with the merger acting as a catalyst for change and improvement. Such circumstances do not tend to be the norm and there is in our view an element of hope over experience in expecting such an outcome.

In our view it is better practice to assess all of the shortcomings identified by the review that identified merger as the most appropriate option to pursue and identify those that will be addressed through merger and those that will not. For the shortcomings identified as not being addressed by merger the fundamental principle is to address them pre- rather than post-merger.

It is also appropriate to expect the same of a merger partner – nobody wishes to inherit other's problems.

As an impetus to addressing such shortcomings there are four factors to bear in mind:

(i) there is real possibility that such shortcomings will jeopardise the merger as understandably any firm will be extremely wary of merging with another with known performance issues;

(ii) addressing the shortcoming will demonstrate to a merger partner that the resolve to confront difficult issues is present in the firm;

(iii) addressing the shortcomings improves the firm's overall competitiveness and hence position in any merger discussions;

(iv) despite best endeavors, any potential merger may not occur (or not occur for a considerable period of time) and so there is a possibility that the issues will have to be dealt with anyway and while they remain unaddressed they will impact adversely on competitiveness.

4

Developing and Assessing the Business Case

In the previous chapter, two frameworks were outlined; the first to assist firms decide whether they should merge and, if so, the second to identify potential merger candidates and then undertake preliminary assessments of their suitability.

Based on these approaches a firm may identify a single potential merger candidate that is clearly superior on initial assessment to all others. Alternatively a number of potential merger candidates might have been identified. If more than one potential merger candidate has been identified it is necessary as a next step to narrow down the options to a single, preferred firm.

Except under genuinely exceptional circumstances it is not realistic to consider entering into negotiations with more than one firm at any one time. This is, in part, because the resources and effort required are greater than any firm can reasonably have and, secondly, because no firm being approached as a potential merger partner is likely to be willing to consider committing the resources to merger discussions if it knows that it is just one of several firms being considered.

Identifying a preferred merger partner

The process of narrowing down a shortlist to a single preferred firm will depend on circumstances. Some 'shortlisted' firms may have no interest in merger whatsoever or no interest in merging with the particular firm that has made the approach or in following a strategy that is in some way at odds with their existing strategic aims.

Each of these circumstances can usually be identified relatively easily and, as outlined previously, initial assessments can be undertaken on a no-name basis by a third party if confidentiality is a particular concern.

At this point there may still be more than a single firm on the shortlist and in these circumstances a further stage of assessment becomes necessary. (Such circumstances are very likely to be the case when seeking to merge in a very large market such as in the US or for smaller firms seeking to merge with a broadly similar sized small firm where the universe of potential candidates even in a relatively modest sized city or region can be large).

This process of assessment is best undertaken using an objective framework although it would be senseless to pretend that more subjective, personality based issues do not play a significant part in the considerations.

Such assessment requires face-to-face meetings between members of the firm seeking to merge and each of the shortlisted firms. The aim of each meeting is to make a judgement of the likely strength of the business case for merger and it is vital for the firm seeking merger that it has a clear set of criteria against which each potential firm can be assessed.

Such criteria may in part be 'objective' and concern factors such as the genuine strength of particular practice areas or offices, the relative size or profitability of each firm, and so on, and in part concern 'softer' issues such as the style of working, 'individual' or team based, the level of ambition and drive, the style of management, the underlying values, and so on.

Our experience is that up to a day should be allowed for each meeting with each shortlisted firm (see Appendix IV for a proposed agenda for such meetings) and that having a framework within which each shortlisted firm can be assessed against pre-specified criteria is highly valuable. See Figure 4.1 for an example of an assessment framework. Score each firm on a 1–5 scale (or otherwise as appropriate) where 1 indicates a low compatibility/strength and 5 a high one.

Inevitably the extent to which the members of the firm seeking merger 'get on' with the members of each shortlisted firm they meet will have a bearing on the overall conclusions of the process but it is important that such considerations are not allowed to dominate the assessment and take on an over-weight importance.

	Firm 1	Firm 2	Firm 3	Firm 4	Firm 5
Criteria 1					
Criteria 2					
Criteria 3					
Criteria 4					
Criteria 5					
Criteria 6					
Criteria 7					
Criteria 8					

Figure 4.1   Assessment Framework

In some cases a number of meetings will be required with each shortlisted firm (or a progressively reducing subset of them) before a single preferred candidate emerges. As part of this process it is important to identify potential 'fatal flaws' and develop a reasonable level of confidence that each can be resolved.

It is important to recognise that merger may not take place with the identified preferred firm and hence it is likely to be important to 'leave the door open' if possible with other firms that do not seem such strong candidates on this initial assessment as it may become desirable to reconsider them if the discussions/negotiations with the preferred firm ultimately do not proceed to merger.

Preparing the business case

Having reached a point where a single preferred merger candidate has been identified, a critically important, and often very poorly undertaken stage of preparation needs to be completed, namely preparing and assessing the strength of the business case for merger with that firm. Assessing the strength of the business case fulfils two purposes – one more obvious, the other, perhaps less so.

The obvious purpose is to evaluate objectively whether merger makes business sense in terms of assisting each firm to achieve its strategic objectives. In this respect the 'business case' is an assessment each party needs to take back to its partnership indicating the extent to which merger advances the firm in pursuit of its strategic aims. To some extent the business case for each party will be different but there would also be an expectation of a very significant level of commonality in the business case for each firm.

The second purpose of developing the business case is to identify, in outline, the critical actions that will need to be taken pre- and in particular post-merger if the merger is to deliver the benefits identified. In this context the business case forms the basis of developing the post-merger integration plan (see Chapter 6) and thereby helps ensure that partners in both firms are aware of the issues that they will need to address and the changes that will be required moving forward post-merger. In this respect the business case highlights what might be regarded as a critical aspect of the 'costs' of merger and is vital in allowing each party to make informed decisions on whether the merger is worth pursuing. It can emerge as a consequence of just such an assessment that for both parties merger can deliver great potential benefits but for one or even both parties the 'costs' of merger represent a downside greater than that partnership is prepared to bear. Such costs could be in terms of literal costs (dollars, euros or pounds) or could be in terms of the changes required in one or both firms such as in the role of partners, the disbandment of certain practice areas, redundancies, conflicts, changes in governance and remuneration, etc.

There are circumstances where the benefits or strategic importance of merger are so great that there is a willingness to bear such costs. In other circumstances there will, rightly, be a baulking at the costs.

As a consequence the firm seeking to merge may turn to another shortlisted firm and explore the strength of the business case there; this would be an entirely valid approach if the identified 'costs' in the previous discussions had been 'firm specific'. Alternatively, the firm seeking merger might decide to abandon thoughts of merger entirely and this is more likely to be the case if the 'costs' are of a 'generic' nature.

Some might argue that abandoning merger because of the 'costs' is a compromise or fudge if previously the strategic rationale for merger had been established. To an extent this argument is valid but surely it is better to abandon merger and rethink one's strategic objectives than to persist with merger in pursuit of those strategic objectives when the 'costs' are considered too high and/or there is no commitment to implementing the actions necessary for merger to deliver the benefits sought of it.

As well as the business case establishing for each firm the potential benefits and implications of merger there is an additional benefit in developing a business case in that it requires partners (and others) from each firm to work together closely in a fairly intensive fashion and thus provides the opportunity for each to asses the other in a far more effective way than simply across a boardroom or hotel table.

The value of developing the business case should not be underestimated and while for smaller firms the development and assessment of the business case for merger may be less important than for larger firms it remains critical. Yet this remains a largely poorly and often superficially executed aspect of merger. Clearly the stronger the business case, and particularly if the business case is strong for both parties, then the more flexibility there is likely to be when negotiating the merger. If 2 plus 2 generates 6 then (at least in theory) there is a potential 50% upside for each firm and there should be a greater willingness (and resource if necessary) to find solutions to difficult issues that arise during negotiations. If, on the other hand 2 plus 2 equals little more than 4 then there is likely to be less inclination and flexibility to find solutions to such issues.

Financial considerations

Before discussing the principles of developing a business case, it is worth commenting on the issues of financial and general performance comparability between potential merger candidates.

There are those, accountants in particular, who argue that at the very outset it is critical to 'sort out' all the financial issues and in particular agree how any differences in profitability will be dealt with. This approach, we would argue, is not the most appropriate in most circumstances and can be quite misguided. Many accountants argue that such issues have to be dealt with at the outset since they are too important to leave aside and are frequently deal breakers making it best not to spend time and invest resources in addressing other issues until these are agreed.

From one perspective the argument is correct in that financial and performance differences have been a breaking point on a number of potential mergers. We would argue, however, that often the reason they have become deal breakers is because of the way they have been addressed upfront and/or because the business case is not that strong. By trying to address these issues at the outset when the business case for merger is not clear it is almost inevitable that they will be a very hard to address.

Certainly one should be aware from the outset if there are significant performance or profitability differences but in our experience it is far more likely that such differences can be satisfactorily addressed if there is a strong business case for merger and if both parties in working on developing the business case have established a strong desire to merge.

Furthermore, an often overlooked factor is that even significant differences in profit can be bridged, at the very least during a transitional post-merger integration period and possibly beyond this, through imaginative approaches to partner compensation.

It is of course the case that significant differences in profitability between firms interested in merging have been and will continue to be insurmountable barriers and, in many circumstances, rightly so because the differences in profitability are a reflection of fundamental differences in the operations, values and underlying work ethic of the two firms. There are, however, circumstances where such differences in profitability are not a reflection of differences in such 'fundamentals' but a consequence of other factors such as the relative competitive nature of the two firms' markets, prevailing fee rates in differing locations or different attitudes towards overall working hours (although no differing attitudes towards client service or quality). In such cases profit differences usually can be bridged and should certainly not automatically be seen as a fatal flaw to merger (except if attempted to be resolved at the outset).

In evaluating financial considerations it is important to review a number of performance indicators (e.g. chargeable and non-chargeable hours, charge-out rates, recovery rates, fees per lawyer and fee earners, fees per partner, overhead levels, profit margins, etc.) and to do so over at least three years. Such analyses provide critical information concerning the 'health' and performance of a firm.

In this context, it is also important to be aware of the converse circumstances where similarities in profits between firms seeking merger are perceived as an indicator of other similarities between the firms. This is a dangerous assumption to make as in reality, it is no indicator of the suitability of two firms merging or necessarily a contributor to the strength of the business case, it is simply a fact that the two firms are similarly profitable at a point in time.

Developing the business case

Developing the business case for merger needs to occur at at least two levels in most cases. At the firmwide level the business case needs to identify how the merging of the two firms will assist in the achieving of agreed strategic objectives; at the second, practice group, level the business case needs to identify how the combination will allow existing clients to be more competitively serviced and new clients/instructions of the type desired won. There may, in addition, be a third level to the business case, namely in the supporting infrastructure. In most cases this level does not have a significant role in the business case although there are exceptions to this and in particular around fee sensitive lower value/commodity focused firms where the combining of infrastructures or the economies of scale that can be achieved through combining two infrastructures are an important contributor to the business case.

It is important that the business case is developed in the context of the changing nature of the marketplace taking into account in particular both trends in the approach clients are taking to buying legal services, their evolving needs and expectations and also the developments (both actual and anticipated) of competitor practices and the impact of this.

This unfortunately is sometimes a missing element in the business case and the focus is too strongly directed at the current situation rather than at the likely needs and expectations of clients and the capabilities of competitors in the future. Inevitably this forward looking focus necessitates a level of prediction about the future and such predictions can of course be either incorrect or invalidated by unanticipated changes in the market and/or the economic, social, political or legal environment. On the other hand, if the predictions are based on the underlying drivers of change in the marketplace (some of which were discussed in Chapter 1) there is an increasing likelihood of their accuracy providing there is no fundamental change in their applicability.

A typical structure of a business case is outlined in the table below although it is important to recognise that circumstances may dictate that an entirely or partially different approach is more appropriate. (An alternative structure is included in Appendix V).

At some point the business case will need to be drafted and so it is useful to have a sense of its likely structure from early on. The development of the business case is likely to require a number of meetings between representatives of the two firms and some of these may take place in parallel with, for example, members of each firm's senior management focusing on the firm level issues while other partners explore the practice group level issues and so on.

It is vital that this process is effectively managed and its overall purpose continually reinforced; otherwise it can easily degenerate into a point scoring exercise. It is critical that the fundamental aim of identifying the potential business case for merger drives the process and while problems, difficulties and differences should not be ignored, neither should they be allowed to bring the process to a premature stalemate or close.

Above all initial friction, tension or even dislike between partners from the two firms must not be allowed to derail the aim of building the business case.

Firm level business case

The starting point for assessing the business case is at the firm level and this needs to be set in the context of the market environment within which the firm expects to be competing. In this context, two sets of factors are particularly important:

- first, a clear view needs to be developed concerning the needs and expectations of core clients and in particular the sort of services they will require, how they will choose to purchase these, how they will expect them to be delivered, what will result in them perceiving value has been delivered, and so on;
- second, a clear and realistic view of the shape of competition is required; who will be the primary competitors for the core clients

Business Case

1. Executive summary
2. Characteristics of market the new firm will be competing in, market trends (or included in appendix)
3. Strategic aims of each firm
4. Agreed strategic aims of combined firm
   - core client types
   - core practice areas
   - value focus
   - basis of competitiveness
5. Overview of each firm and 'forecast' overview of combined firm on proposed effective date of merger:
   - size
   - fee income
   - client base
   - economics
   - position in market
   - key competitors
6. Summary of opportunities created in each practice area through merger
   - overview of each major practice area in combined firm
   - opportunities with existing clients e.g. cross-sell new services, service in new locations
   - potential to attract new clients e.g. larger clients, clients with more diversified needs
7. Degree of 'cultural' fit
8. Opportunities created through combination of infrastructures
9. Initial identification of critical steps needed to realise benefits
   - people integration
   - marketing
   - core client management
   - etc.
10. Identified costs of merger
    - direct merger costs
    - continuing costs
11. Forecast impact on economics and overall profitability
    - key performance indicators
    - margin
    - forecast PPEP
12. Potential obstacles to merger
    - conflict
    - differences in values, attitudes, philosophies
    - differences in management style
    - differences in the role of partners and level of autonomy
    - differences in approach to partner remuneration, capital funding, etc.

and services, what will be their capabilities, what strengths do they each have, what, if any, are their weaknesses, and so on.

It is within this context that the strategy for the new firm needs to be both developed and assessed:

- what will constitute the core client types of the new firm;
- what will be the core services;
- what will be the value focus;
- what will be the basis of the new firm's competitiveness.

The validity of the strategy needs to be assessed objectively in the context of the market environment within which the new firm expects to compete. In particular the focus needs to be on the consideration of what the new firm will need to be able to offer clients and prospects in order to be perceived as genuinely competitive rather than merely competent.

This analysis may indicate, for example, that at the point of merger the new firm will not be 'one of the leaders' in a particular market sector which is a strategic aim of the merger. In practice such an outcome is quite likely to be the case since simply bringing together two firms rarely achieves more in the first instance than creating a larger firm, perhaps with greater geographic coverage. In such circumstances the next step needs to be an identification of the steps that will have to be taken to make the new firm more competitive. The likelihood of achieving such steps also needs to be considered. Are they realistic given the background, history and capabilities of each firm? What steps might competitor firms take to outperform the new firm and so on?

In particular, it is important to recognise that merger does not automatically induce any changes in behaviour. If, for example, neither firm considering merger has a strong record of cross-selling then why should this start occurring in the new firm? Similarly, if neither firm has a strong track-record in new business development, is it realistic to expect the new firm to be strongly committed and focused on new business development? Hence, if the success of a particular merger requires extensive cross-selling or new business development but the above circumstances have historically prevailed, there are perhaps indications of hope over realistic expectation and a further consideration of the validity of merger is indicated.

Personality issues begin to take on a greater significance at this point and those exploring the strength of the business case are inevitably making judgements about their 'opposite numbers'. What is important to try and establish is whether such concerns are in essence personality based or reflect deeper differences in values, attitudes and philosophies. Clearly, personality clashes or differences are likely to impact on the ease with which a business case is explored but should not, per se, be considered a fundamental block to a business case except if they are of such an extreme nature that they make it pretty much impossible for people to sit in the same room together.

On the other hand, differences in values, attitudes and philosophies can be more significant obstacles; of course it can be quite the reverse and one or both firms is deliberately seeking to merge with another with a different approach in order to shift its internal environment. (Whether such a merger would act as a catalyst is questionable and it might have the converse affect with partners from each legacy firm clinging more closely to type).

Inevitably there is also here a degree of 'jockeying for position' either overtly or beneath the surface. Again, this is unavoidable and particularly the case if one or both firms have partners in leadership and management positions who are concerned about their future positions. In the world of corporate mergers there have been a number of high profile cases where merger has not taken place despite a strong business case because of apparently irresolvable differences over leadership of the merged entity. In such circumstances the influence – either openly or covertly – of major outside shareholders is often bought to bear and increasingly pension funds and other institutional investors have demonstrated their intolerance for allowing such issues to prevent a merger proceeding particularly if the shareholder value-added through merger is forecast to be significant.

Unfortunately perhaps in the case of law firm mergers, such external, more level-headed intervention is not present; perhaps also, somewhat disingenuously, the real reasons for mergers not occurring in such circumstances is disguised and the issues of disagreement over future 'leadership' are dressed up in terms of fundamental 'differences in culture' or 'strategy' or the like. Perhaps, however, with external funding and third-party ownership of law firms at some point in the future the type of pressure external shareholders have applied to public corporates will be brought to bear on law firms.

The reality is that on a rational basis such issues should not be allowed to become a significant factor in the business case and again this is an area where external advisers can play an invaluable role in ensuring such issues do not assume a disproportionate importance.

Ultimately the issue of leadership and management of the new firm is essentially a matter for merger discussions rather than a key aspect of the business case. And in this context, as we discuss in the next chapter, decisions should be taken on the basis of what is in the best interests of the new firm and maximising its chances of success and competitiveness rather than being driven by the concerns of individual partners and their personal positions in the management of the new firm. Underlying all of this can be concerns by both firms that they are seen as the dominant party in the new firm or to ensure that there is no perception – either internally or in the market – that they have been 'acquired' or taken over. These concerns also tend to be inevitable and unavoidable but again should not be allowed to dominate the merger process. To do otherwise risks passing by excellent merger opportunities and if this is to be the case partners have to be prepared to live with the consequences.

Clearly if at the firm-level the business case for merger appears weak there is little likelihood of there being value in proceeding to explore the strength of the business case at the practice group level. Either way a report back to the partnership at this point is probably appropriate indicating the basis of the business case or the reasons for there being little sense in pursuing with discussions.

Assuming that a strong business case does appear to exist it will probably make sense to prepare a paper for circulation and discussion with partners at this point outlining the potential benefits that merger could deliver and any obvious drawbacks. Drafting such a paper serves two purposes:

1) first, the very process of preparing the paper necessitates clarifying in an objective way what benefits merger might deliver;

2) second, it fulfils a key communication role in terms of keeping partners aware of progress and importantly, on the basis of this allows them to 'test', hopefully in a constructive way, the strength of the case.

Practice level business case

The second level of the business case is at the practice group level. Here the aim is to bring together in a series of meetings the partners from the key practice groups of each firm to identify the level of overlap or complementarity in the respective practice groups and the opportunities that combination might create both in terms of better servicing (or defending) existing clients and winning new clients/instructions of a type consistent with the agreed outline strategy of the new firm.

Depending on the nature of the firms considering merger such meetings should not be restricted simply to the similar practice groups and it may be appropriate to have meetings of partners focused on particular industry sectors or even specific clients with again the aim being to ascertain how a combined firm might improve (or defend) its position within specific industry sectors or with specific clients. For example, if one firm has a particular strength in IP and IT and the other in Corporate work but both focused on a broadly similar client base then one appropriate approach to evaluating merger opportunities is likely to be on an industry sector or client type basis.

During these meetings there are inevitably underlying issues of personal chemistry and sometimes also considerations of management, power and position in a merged firm, and so on. The danger is that such issues become the focus rather than the business issues.

To prevent this from occurring, it is often advisable at least during the initial set of meetings between practice groups to have members of each firm's senior management present to keep the discussions on the agenda. Alternatively, if outside advisers are involved this is a useful function that they can fulfil. Inevitably issues of individuals' position, authority and influence in the merged firm will be in partners' minds; it would be naïve to think otherwise and understandably these are very real concerns. Such issues do indeed need to be addressed but in our mind they should not have a significant influence on the strength or otherwise of the business case unnecessarily.

One issue to guard against in particular at this point is negative judgements about individual partners in the other firm scuppering a business case. Such negative judgements are usually based on either personal issues (intense dislike – possibly as a consequence of previous dealings) or concerns over professional capability or integrity. Such issues do have to be addressed but again should not be allowed to destroy or undermine a business case except it there is a conclusive argument backed up with genuine evidence.

Issues of professional capability or integrity are very serious but they need examining in an objective and unemotional light and initial judgements may prove to be quite incorrect. Unfortunately, however, marketplace perceptions in respect of professional capability and integrity cannot be ignored and even if such perceptions are not supported by the evidence they can still destroy a business case.

Personal issues are a rather different matter and ultimately tend to be articulated in terms of *'I could never work in the same practice group or firm as X'* or *'I could never be a partner of Y'*. In smaller firm mergers such sentiment can destroy a business case but even in such circumstances it is important to understand what is beneath such sentiment and what if anything could be done to address it. And it has to be recognised that if such sentiment is a reflection of the stance of only one or two partners, the loss of such partners and the impact of this may have to be considered.

In larger firm mergers there is statistically a greater likelihood (simply because of the numbers of partners involved) of some intense issues of personal dislike or contempt arising. This has to be accepted and then addressed and managed in an effective way. It may mean that one or more partners from one or both firms ultimately has to leave and the issue then becomes one of considering whether such an eventuality would totally undermine the business case or is so strongly counter to the values of the firms that irrespective of the impact it effectively acts as a veto to proceeding.

The practice group meetings need to have a clear objective and focus and one way of achieving this is to request that the partners produce an outline business plan for the combined practice group indicating what the aims would be and what would need to be achieved to realise such aims. An agenda for such practice group meetings is included in Appendix VI and this agenda is designed to have as an output an initial, summary level practice group business plan based on the two firms merging.

Cultural fit

In parallel with the practice group meetings occurring, the issue of 'cultural fit' between the two firms needs to be assessed. This tends to be one of the most poorly addressed issues in law firm mergers and at its most superficial, and unfortunately far too commonly, consists of little more than partners of the two firms meeting informally together over drinks and seeing how they get on. Whether one does or does not get on at a cocktail party is largely an irrelevance and is certainly no real test of 'cultural fit'. Cultural fit can be tested although it is a complex issue and it is important that more superficial similarities between firms and their partners are not regarded as 'proof' of cultural fit.

This is a matter where experienced external advisers can contribute in a very valuable way. The critical issue here tends not to be so much one of seeking a perfect match in terms of culture, values or internal environment but being aware of more significant differences and considering whether they do constitute a potential fatal flaw in the business case for merger or alternatively how they can be managed and/or become a source of additional strength in the new firm.

For example, if the two firms do have somewhat different, but fundamentally not incompatible, styles of working then the combined firm may be stronger in terms of being able to offer a broader choice to clients. Similarly it may be possible to manage the integration of the differences in culture to create something stronger than either of the legacy firms has.

Key indicators to consider with regard to culture include:

- the role and authority of management;
- the role and autonomy of partners;
- the style of behaviour and working – individual or team based;
- the relationship between the lawyers and central support staff – hierarchical (master-servant) or egalitarian (collaboration of equals);
- the approach to partner remuneration – open or closed, prospective or retrospective, performance based or lockstep and, if the former, the prime criteria taken into account;

- policy on partner drawings and profit distribution;
- levels or otherwise of internal competitiveness;
- productivity expectations of partners and assistants – hours, fees generated;
- commitment to training, development of assistants, career planning;
- approach to marketing – integrated, and managed at firm/ practice group level or largely dependent on individual initiative and commitment;
- commitment to pro-bono work and community;
- diversity of partnership – homogeneous or heterogeneous;
- relative importance of financial, professional and personal objectives;
- financing of the firm – level of borrowing and of partners' capital accounts.

Infrastructure compatibility and synergies

As indicated previously, it is relatively unusual for a merger to generate significant additional competitiveness through the combination of two firms' infrastructures. Similarly it is unusual for the combination of the two infrastructures to raise significant genuine hurdles (although the costs of integrating IT systems can be significant). There will, however, inevitably be concerns over who will get the 'top jobs' in the new firm and whether redundancies will occur. Nevertheless, there are cases where the combination of infrastructures can generate genuine additional competitiveness and thus contribute to the overall business case and so it is important to assess as part of the business case the implications of bringing the two firms together from an infrastructure perspective.

In particular it is important to focus on potential IT costs should the two firms' systems be incompatible; this might be with regard to any or all of practice management software, accounting systems, document and knowledge management, the underlying operating platforms, and so on.

Critical success issues

Having examined the business case at each of the firm, practice group and infrastructure level and also considered the level of cultural fit, there should be a clear identification of the critical issues that will need to be addressed in order for the merger to 'deliver' the benefits hoped of it. There are likely to be a number of critical issues emerging – typically related to a number of areas including:

(i) management and organisation;
(ii) people integration into new enlarged practice groups;
(iii) achieving work style consistency (so that clients experience a one-firm approach);
(iv) effective client management;
(v) marketing and business development to win the target clients determined by the new firm's strategy;
(vi) performance expectations.

It is important to identify these critical issues for three reasons in particular:

- first, so that an objective assessment can be made as to whether it is realistic to expect the new firm to be able and committed to address such issues. Quite simply, given the history, track record, culture and capabilities of each of the legacy firms, is it realistic to expect the new firm to address effectively each?;
- secondly, it is important to identify in broad terms the costs of addressing the issues, netting any savings that are expected;
- thirdly, identifying the implications as part of the business case is a critical aspect of managing overall expectations. Partners need to understand the implications of merger and will naturally be concerned to understand what it will mean to them as individuals, both as owners of the new firm and in terms of their day to day working.

Initial financial assessment

Having completed this assessment it should be possible to undertake initial evaluations to identify the financial implications of merger both in terms of costs and the likely economics of the new firm.

The costs assessment should focus on both the actual cost of merger and the ongoing costs (or possibly savings) the new firm will carry. The cost of merger will include obvious items such as the fees of professional advisers, integration costs, cost of integrating practice management, IT and accounts systems, the development and implementation of a new brand identity (except if one firm is assuming the other's existing identity), costs of new premises and/or moving costs, travel and meeting costs, etc.

Other merger costs are more difficult to ascertain as they concern issues such as loss of productivity in terms of utilisation levels. Inevitably merger discussions are a distraction from the normal fee earning activities of partners; as well as the to be expected loss of productivity of those most heavily involved in guiding the merger through its various stages the possibility of some loss of productivity among a wider group of partners and also other fee earners and support staff is likely. Apart from time spent in merger related meetings, planning and consultation, the uncertainty created by merger is a distraction with each and every individual concerned to a greater or lesser extent about the impact it will have on them personally; in such circumstances, particularly if rumours start circulating about possible redundancies or internal disagreements or some partners contemplating jumping ship, then there will be an almost inevitable increase in 'corridor gossip' and decrease in productivity.

The issue of communication, both internal and external, is addressed in the next chapter, but clearly managing this properly is key to help prevent the fact that merger is being considered becoming a more significant distraction and cost than needs be or, even worse, a destabilising factor.

In this respect, the impact of merger discussions can be particularly concerning for those just outside the equity. In particular many of them will be understandably concerned about the impact that merger may have on their prospects for admission to equity. Managing this situation carefully is important and while it may be neither feasible nor appropriate to keep such individuals fully informed of each development, there are real risks if they are not kept in the loop or if they feel an uninformed, unvalued 'pawn' in the process.

The risks are that such individuals can create, either inadvertently or deliberately, discontent in the firm and/or depart. Moreover, headhunters and competitor firms are all aware of the somewhat destabilising impact of uncertainty created by the possibility of merger and in today's highly competitive market will not hesitate in attempting to take advantage of such a situation.

Other costs (certainly in cash flow terms) include issues such as the possible requirement to pay tax liabilities caused by the dissolution of one or both partnerships or even a change in financial year-ends. There are also apparent costs in bringing together firms where one operates on a cash basis and the other on an accruals basis. It can be argued that some such 'costs' have in fact been incurred unrelated to merger but are simply crystallised by merger. Irrespective of such arguments, such liabilities are likely to be seen as 'costs' of merger and understandably partners will want to see that such costs are more than offset by the benefits of merger.

Forecasting the economics of the new firm is an area open to 'creative' and not generally particularly helpful forecasting. In the majority of mergers a forecast of an increase of, say, just 5% in rates or productivity can be demonstrated to offset the costs of merger, and sometimes several times over. And those in favour of merger will argue that merger 'cannot fail' to deliver benefits of this modest level at an absolute minimum. The same people are also likely to argue that savings of at least 5% in the aggregate of the two legacy firms' overhead costs must also be achievable; this too, it will be pointed out, will drop straight through to the bottom line boosting profit per partner. In practice either or both of the above may occur. Equally likely, however, they may not in the period immediately proceeding merger and a conservative approach to constructing forecasts for the merged firm is strongly recommended – better by far to have an unexpected post-merger financial upside rather than downside.

In particular realism, based on experience, is a sensible approach to follow in developing initial forecasts and budgets as part of the business case. Our experience is consistent on three issues in particular:

1) Clients are discerning and sophisticated as purchasers of legal services and are likely to be on guard against rate increases. A bigger firm, created through merger, cannot charge higher fees simply as a consequence of its increased size. Hence, except if there is clear evidence and a supporting argument to the contrary it is best not to assume in forecasting or budgeting that rates can be increased. Unfortunately in a number of cases optimistic and unrealistic increases in fee rates are built into budgets and the failure to realise these is significant.

2) Selling additional services to existing clients of either legacy firm takes time to materialise. Even if the due diligence (see Chapter 5) indicates that core clients of one or both of the legacy firms are willing or likely to buy more extensively from an enlarged firm with greater capabilities such intentions do not tend to materialise immediately. Clients will tend to want to see the new firm settled down post-merger (being aware of the time it takes two firms to integrate effectively) prior to entrusting it with a significantly greater volume or breadth of instructions. Furthermore, it is important to recognise that winning a greater level of instructions from existing clients or indeed winning instructions from new clients means taking the work off other, competitor firms. This takes time and persistence and an ability to demonstrate that the new firm has a capability and competitiveness over and above that of the incumbent provider. Again experience here shows that this all takes time and this should be factored into any forecasts and budgets.

3) Savings in overheads do not tend to be significant and especially so in the first year or so of merger except under special circumstances such as where one firm can leave its premises with no ongoing liabilities and move into surplus space of its merger partner. Savings in support staff tend to be minimal initially and while the combined firm won't require, say, two finance directors or two IT directors it will, most probably, require more experienced finance and IT directors due to the increasing complexity of the remits and will also, most likely, have to pay higher salaries for senior support staff because of the greater responsibilities of the positions. Indeed overhead costs of the new firm may be higher than the aggregate of the legacy practices. Again, except if the evidence shows to the contrary it is realistic, certainly for the initial period post-merger, to assume limited if any savings in overhead and quite possibly additional costs.

Given the above it will be no surprise that the implications of merger in financial terms tend to be neutral at best and, more often than not, impact negatively on profit margins and profit per partner, ceteris paribus, in the first year or years of merger.

Clearly if merger takes place during a period of rising demand for legal services or in a generally buoyant market then such costs may get offset by increases in fee income that result from the prevailing market conditions. Experience shows, however, that in the majority of circumstances, having stripped out the effects of changing market conditions, mergers tend to impact neutrally or negatively on profit in the initial period post-merger.

Of course there are exceptions to this, but a very careful review of the assumptions behind any forecasts showing a significant increase in profit post-merger is advisable. The reality is the costs of merger both those relating to the merger itself and then increases to the cost-base of the enlarged firm impact from the outset whereas the benefits take time to flow through both in terms of the economies that arise through more cost-effective and/or efficient operations and the increase in rates and/or volume of work that arise from offering better services to clients and/or a wider range of services.

Identifying potential show stoppers

The final aspect of developing the business case is to identify the potential hurdles to merger and the implications of these. The early stages of work on the business case should hopefully have identified any 'fatal flaws' but typical issues that may have arisen during the course of reviewing the strength of the business case include:

- client conflicts;
- appointments to senior management positions;
- fundamental differences in the type and style of management;
- differences in approaches to partner remuneration and/or partnership funding;
- differences in the role and performance expectations of partners;
- differences in values, attitudes and philosophies between the firms.

The issue of conflict is complex, particularly when merger between large, broadly complementary firms is being considered; some conflicts are likely. Such conflicts may be genuine legal conflicts in terms of ongoing litigation or acting for opposing parties in a deal or on an ongoing basis. Often, more common, are conflicts that are essentially commercial in that clients of one firm or other would not be prepared to continue to instruct the firm should merger occur because this would result in a competitor of theirs also being a client of the new firm. Major car, food and beverage manufacturers, for example, tend to prefer their lawyers not to act for any competitors and the same is true in other large consolidated industries such as telecoms, tobacco and petrochemicals.

Of course such conflicts can also occur with small scale regional mergers where, for example, real estate developers may have concerns if a merger would result in the new firm also acting for a major competitor.

The critical point at this stage is not to try and resolve the issues but to flag them up so that in assessing the strength of the business case as complete a picture as possible of both the benefits and the drawbacks of a proposed merger can be considered.

Throughout the period of assessing the strength of the business case periodic reviews should take place in order to ensure that the process is on track and on timetable and that both firms, based on the evidence gathered and assessed to date, believe that the exercise is worth continuing. On this basis fatal flaws and/or the weight of evidence being against merger will tend to come out earlier rather than at the stage of actually drafting a report on the business case.

Involvement of external advisers

There tends to be value in involving outside advisers in the process of developing a business case: this can be one set of advisers jointly instructed by both firms or alternatively each firm may prefer to have its own advisers. Obviously the prime role such advisers play will vary accordingly to circumstances but typically will include many or all of the following:

- managing the process of developing and assessing the strength of the business case;
- undertaking necessary research and analysis;
- preparing periodic progress reports and final reports;
- providing an independent opinion on the strength of the business case;
- mediating and/or helping find ways forward on difficult issues;
- keeping the process to time constraints;

- helping address 'emotional' issues;
- providing executive, administrative and secretarial capabilities.

Perhaps one of the key values of involving external advisers in this part of the process is that for many lawyers developing a business case is relatively unfamiliar ground. Lawyers tend to have significant experience in handling negotiations but this tends to occur after their clients have established the strength of the business case for a particular transaction.

Experience shows that without external assistance the process of developing and assessing the business case is either covered only superficially or alternatively becomes somewhat adversarial, more akin to negotiating rather than an objective exercise realistically identifying and assessing any drawbacks and hurdles but primarily focusing on the benefits and upside that merger could realise.

As a final step in this stage of the process, the strength of the business case needs to be assessed by each partnership and a decision made as to whether to proceed or not. As part of this assessment each party is likely to hold partners' meetings and engage in a process of consultation; included in this 'representatives' of each firm's management may address the other firm's partners and participate in smaller group meetings of partners.

Typically the process of developing and assessing a business case will take anything from 4 weeks upwards depending on the size and complexity of the firms involved, the level of resources each firm commits to the process and the priority afforded.

5
Merger Negotiations

Preparations for negotiations

Prior to merger negotiations commencing both firms will require a mandate from their partnership to proceed. This mandate, based on the strength of the business case, in effect establishes that both partnerships are clear that merger represents the most effective (or only) way of achieving their strategic objectives.

There will be some occasions where such partnership support is based on unequivocal, enthusiastic commitment; partners are excited and eager to merge perceiving it as an opportunity to realise ambitions that cannot be achieved otherwise and having few if any reservations about their preferred merger partners at either a collective or individual level. In other circumstances the commitment to merge may be more restrained: there is perhaps a clear acceptance of the benefits of merger but, in parallel, a deep-seated preference that the firm's strategic aims could be achieved without the need to merge. Put another way, there is an acceptance that merger is a necessity given the strategic aims but nevertheless a wish that some other means of realising these aims existed.

Irrespective of the circumstances there has to be a genuine commitment to merger from both sides before detailed merger negotiations should begin. This does not mean that either or both firms are giving carte blanche to those negotiating the merger nor are they giving a mandate to merge at any cost. There should, however, be a mandate provided to each firm's negotiating team by their respective partnerships, containing, as appropriate, an indication of the 'limits' to which negotiations can proceed without reverting to the partnership or the firm's management. Such a mandate is however a very different situation from what can occur where a significant number of partners in one or both firms have substantive reservations about the proposed merger and so impose severe constraints on those negotiating on their behalf so that the chances of a merger occurring are reduced to practically zero.

This is not a realistic position to start from – better by far not to commence merger negotiations than to begin them with such significant constraints because of the concerns of a group of partners. Differences of view between partners need to be sorted out prior to the discussions beginning rather than jeopardising the entire process; the destabilising impact of the merger discussions breaking down because of a perception by one group of partners that another group of partners has undermined the prospect of merger by placing unrealistic constraints on the process are likely to be severe. They may even be catastrophic in terms of that firm's future viability with deep divides and schisms rife and a likelihood of significant resignations, damaging political infighting or even break-up occurring.

In some circumstances a mandate is actually drafted and those leading the discussions have clear instructions from their partnerships on particular issues – sometimes just a few, sometimes a considerable number. In other circumstances no such formal mandate exists and those leading the discussions have no formal constraints placed on them. In such circumstances there are in many respects greater burdens on the negotiators in that under each issue being negotiated there is a need to make a judgement in terms of the balance between what the other firm wants, what is in the interest of the long term competitiveness of the new firm and what one's own partners will accept.

Clearly each party should communicate any non-negotiables to the other side and these should be considered prior to negotiations commencing as part of the business case considerations. In this respect there can be considered to be formal constraints on certain issues. In most respects however it tends to be better for those involved in negotiations not to be burdened with specific constraints on a multitude of issues as this can significantly hamper both the flexibility and timings of the discussions.

Better by far to have those involved in the discussions being partners who have the respect and trust of their respective partnerships
to move forward on the negotiations as they see fit and be confident
that on the sensitive issues they will have a strong sense of what
outcomes would be acceptable to their respective partnerships and
what outcomes would not.

Hence, while there are of course exceptions, as a general rule it
tends to be better for those negotiating the merger to be fully aware
of the sentiment in their partnership and base negotiations on this
rather than having an overly constraining mandate or have to
report back to their partnership on many points for instruction.

Underlying principles of negotiations

Before discussing the make up of the team that should lead and
manage the merger discussions and their remit it is important to
make two key points.

The first is that the underlying mindset of both firms throughout
the merger discussions should be to reach conclusions and negotiate
agreements not on the basis of what is in the best interests of the
partners in their own firm but on the basis of what is in the best
interests of the new firm in terms of maximising its overall competitiveness and chances of achieving the agreed strategic aims. This
can be a difficult mindset for lawyers to adopt since their normal
position on negotiating transactions is to achieve the best possible
outcome for their client; the approach that is needed in negotiating
mergers between law firms is subtly but importantly different.

This should not be taken to imply that there will not be a need for
hard negotiating, compromise and even a degree of horse-trading
but ultimately if a successful outcome is to be achieved (both in
terms of completing the merger and maximising the longer term
prospects of the merged firm) then the overriding consideration has
to be one of protecting one's own firm and partners' interests but in
the context of reaching agreements that are in the best interests of
the new firm.

This leads to the second important issue that should underlie the
merger discussions and this is that one is negotiating with one's
potential future partners rather than, say, with owners of a business
that, post-merger, one will not have to deal or work with again as

tends to be the case with many corporate mergers. This is not the occasion for point scoring or 'grinding down' the other side into capitulation. As indicated in the paragraph above this does not mean that there is no place for tough negotiations but ultimately if success is achieved the other firm's negotiators will shortly be your partners and it is important that the launch of the new firm is not compromised by tactics used and positions taken during merger discussions or, worse still, one side withdraws from the discussions entirely because of the behaviour of negotiators from the other firm.

Composition of the negotiating team

A key issue for each firm to settle at the outset is the composition of its merger negotiation team. In many cases the composition of the team may be largely influenced by the success or otherwise of the team that developed and evaluated the strength of the business case. If there is a perception that they handled this process effectively, they have the confidence of their partners and have formed good working relationships with their opposite numbers then this group may be the obvious choice to lead the negotiations.

Of course it may be that this team does not have the appropriate experience and skills to lead the negotiations: they may have been well suited to establish and assess the case for merger and identify the most promising merger candidate but not have the prerequisite skills (or possibly time) to lead the actual negotiations. Obviously if this is the case then a different team will be required but it is generally worth ensuring at least a degree of overlap between those involved in the early stages and developing the business case and those undertaking the negotiations. Without this, continuity in the process is lost along with momentum and there is a loss of the benefit of the working relationships established. It can of course be argued that those who have worked closely on the business case will not be as objective as others in the negotiations and while this may be true in some circumstances it is inappropriate to consider it a 'generic fault' in having the same team who developed the business case continue with the process of negotiating the merger.

In practice in most cases there tends to be a negotiating team comprising a mix of the team that developed the business case (which is beneficial from the perspective of continuity, relationships and momentum) and some new members bringing in fresh-blood, an objective, independent perspective and the necessary skills and experience to undertake the negotiations.

In some circumstances the negotiating team is largely or exclusively comprised of members of the firm's management and/or other senior partners in the firm. This is often appropriate but there can be circumstances where it is more appropriate to appoint a separate negotiating team and then the firm's senior management can act as a valuable independent group that the negotiating team can turn to seek guidance, test ideas, and so on. Moreover, the firm's management can then also provide a useful 'checks and balance' oversight ensuring that progress is in line with expectations and that negotiations remain focused on achieving an outcome in line with the fundamental strategic objectives of the merger.

In addition the management can be called upon as a 'superior' group to help find 'solutions' to any issues that the negotiating team have found impossible to resolve.

If the management group or a subset of it forms the negotiating team then this opportunity does not exist but this may not be important and in many firms it is likely to be considered quite inappropriate for anyone but the firm's management to lead the negotiations.

The most appropriate advice to give on this issue is at least to think carefully through the pros and cons of different compositions of the merger negotiation team and take soundings from the partnership before making any final decision.

Irrespective of their roles in the firm (management or non-management) members of the negotiation task force need to have the following characteristics and capabilities:

- have an in depth understanding of and be actively committed to the realisation of the firm's strategic goals;
- be committed to the merger but to not be of the school of 'merger at any cost';
- be respected both within their own practice group and more widely across the firm;
- have a keen sense of what would be acceptable to the partnership;
- have the confidence of the partnership to negotiate on its behalf;
- have well developed negotiating skills;
- have time to devote to the negotiations.

A mix of senior and less senior partners may be advantageous, in part because of their differing perspectives and the number of years they are likely to have to live with the outcome of the negotiations and in part because the peer group of each within the firm is likely to be different. While not necessarily a critical issue in considering the composition of the negotiating team it is useful to bear in mind that there will be significant management and integration tasks to be undertaken post-merger and it may be important, in order to ensure continuity, that members of the negotiating team are in a position to assume some such responsibilities if that emerges as appropriate.

In larger firms there is more likely to be a suitable cadre of partners involved in management from whom the inclination may be to select the merger negotiation team. As indicated, this may be quite appropriate but nevertheless thought should be given to the potential benefits of bringing other partners into the team, possibly including identified potential future leaders of the firm.

The issue of the time commitment required of members of the negotiating team should not be underestimated. (Perhaps a useful guide here is to estimate the longest possible period of time it might require and triple it!). This means that members of the negotiating team need to have support and cover for their normal client work and possibly other responsibilities from colleagues; without this it is virtually inevitable that the merger discussions will be repeatedly delayed as one member or another of the negotiating team gets called away by client demands that only that particular partner can address. Not only does this mean that time targets get missed but it also jeopardises the entire process with momentum being lost and one firm potentially perceiving the other firm's lack of ability to focus on the negotiations as a sign of lack of commitment.

The ideal number of members on the negotiating team will depend on a number of factors including the anticipated complexity of the merger and at a more pragmatic level the number of partners who have the prerequisite skills and capabilities and can make time for the task. Generally speaking a team of c.2–4 seems the most effective size as the core team with other members co-opted to assist on specific tasks or alternatively specific aspects delegated to small sub teams to address and report back on to the core team.

Having indicated what experience shows to be the 'ideal', it is important to stress that successful mergers have also been agreed with as few as one 'negotiator' on each side and also involving far larger core teams.

In some circumstances the core team addresses every issue, taking the entire task on themselves; in other circumstances they assume a role that is essentially that of leading and managing the process within broad terms that they have agreed and with much of the detailed work and negotiations delegated to a number of task forces, some or all of which may need or choose to use the services of external advisers.

Structuring the discussions

In effect there are two related but separate sets of issues being addressed in merger negotiations and timing considerations tend to dictate that they need to take place broadly in parallel if the merger negotiations are not to drag out too long.

(i) One set of issues concerns the actual terms of the merger and will tend to focus on issues of ownership, financial integration, leadership and management of the new firm, and so on. In a nutshell they are concerned with the process of bringing the two legacy firms together and the constitution or partnership deed under which the new firm will then operate. Typically included here will be issues such as:

- Partnership structure;
- Governance, management structure, decision making and voting;
- Consolidation issues, including financial, accounting and tax implications;
- Capital/funding requirements;
- Merging the two firms' balance sheets and profit & loss account issues;
- Partner remuneration/profit sharing;
- Appointments, retirements and dismissals;
- Organisational structure;
- Expected performance contributions at each level in the new firm;

- Name;
- Transitional arrangements;
- Appointments to key positions.

(ii) The other set of issues is concerned with setting policies for the new firm and ensuring that it operates effectively and efficiently. Typical issues here include:

- Developing the detail of the new firm's strategy;
- Combining the two firms' IT systems;
- Establishing a common approach to client management;
- Establishing common work processes and documentation to be utilised in each practice group;
- Establishing equity partner admission criteria;
- Establishing a common approach to the recruitment, training and development of legal and administrative staff;
- Establishing a common approach to marketing and business development;
- Establishing a common approach to accounting;
- Premises issues.

Partner consultation and communication

The negotiating teams will obviously operate within the remits and mandates from their respective partnerships with their overall objective being to establish an agreement that maximises the competitiveness of the new firm and which is acceptable to both firms.

Larger firms

A key issue almost always is the level of authority and discretion delegated to the negotiating team. In very large firms this tends to be more extensive. In part this is out of necessity but also tends to be a reflection of the way larger firms operate with more extensive levels of delegation.

In many large firms management will have a 'permanent remit' to explore merger opportunities as they arise without a requirement to consult with the partnership and most certainly without any need to get a specific mandate from partners. In some circumstances in larger firms there may be little if any consultation or communication with partners (except on a selected, need to know basis) until the terms of the merger are essentially agreed. This is particularly likely to be the case if, say, issues of confidentiality are critical. Also if management is highly trusted by partners and has partners' confidence then there may be less reason to consult earlier: management will have the trust of the partnership to be always acting in the overall interests of the firm and there will be an underlying assumption that any proposal or recommendation that management put to the partnership will be in the partnership's overall best interests.

If however, the implications of the merger are very far reaching then, even in a large firm, there is likely to be a requirement to involve partners in consultation from fairly early on to give them time to consider and participate in the process. Except in extraordinary circumstances, presenting partners with a radical merger recommendation with little forewarning or prior consultation is likely to result in a significant proportion of partners questioning or even rejecting the proposal. In part this will be a consequence of the conservative, cautious side of many lawyers coming to bear on the circumstances and in part a form of 'snub' to management indicating disquiet at their lack of consultation and perceived disregard of the need to have this. As always circumstances will dictate the point that management will judge it is appropriate to consult with the partnership irrespective of the delegated formal authority it has.

Smaller firms

Interestingly in small firms the issue of the authority and discretion delegated to the negotiating team tends to be relatively less complex. In part this is because in smaller firms issues of communication and confidentiality are easier to handle. Also in small firm mergers the overall negotiations can tend to be less complex and it is highly likely that the negotiating team will comprise the more influential members of each firm; while there will need to be a formal endorsement of any agreement there is, in reality, through a mix of influence, power, and/or trust a relatively high likelihood of anything recommended by the negotiating team being agreed, primarily because of its composition.

In some very small firms the actual negotiations may be handled by a single partner and this can be very effective (both in terms of the actual negotiations and in allowing other partners to continue with all important client work and fee earning). It does, however, require that the partnership has a very high level of trust in that individual and confidence that the recommendations he puts to the partnership are the 'best' that can be achieved.

In this context, 'best' needs to be seen both from the perspective of the existing partnership and in terms of the future success of the new firm; the two are clearly at times in potential conflict or at least not necessarily identical. For example, agreeing significant annuities for retiring partners may be seen as a 'good deal' for such individuals and 'buy' their commitment to merge; on the other hand it may significantly compromise the future profitability of the new firm and thereby impact adversely, and possibly damagingly so, on its future competitiveness. Clearly there are trade-offs and judgements to be made in such circumstances and it is in respect of the 'calls' on such matters that partners must have the confidence in the individual (or individuals) negotiating on their behalf.

Of course there should be consultation on such sensitive issues along the way to ensure that what is being discussed is acceptable in overall terms but it is not realistic to then expect it to be possible to re-open negotiations, not because the terms are unacceptable but because of a sense that a 'better deal' is possible or should/could have been negotiated.

Mid-size firms

It is often in mid-size firms that there is the greater challenge in deciding the terms of the authority and discretion of the negotiating team and the levels of consultation required. There can also be an added challenge in such firms in that the partnership deed requires a very high percentage and sometimes even unanimous partnership agreement to merger for it to occur.

In such circumstances it may be advisable to explore the possibility of amending the partnership deed in this respect prior to merger discussions commencing; this is a sensitive issue and it is important that it is recognised that the change (likely reduction) in the level of support required to proceed with merger is not seen as an attempt to 'railroad' through a merger against the wishes of a minority (poss-ibly very small) of partners but a reflection of the changing en-vironment that law firms operate within that makes it impossible to move forward with total consensus on every issue.

One of the particular issues in mid-size firms is that they some-times tend to be somewhat less advanced in their development in terms of their willingness to delegate to management: this may be largely a timing issue – a reflection of the fact that it takes time for partners to become comfortable delegating significant authority to management and so it can be a consequence of the fact that such levels of confidence have not yet been reached. Alternatively, it may be a more fundamental philosophical matter in that there is a culture of limited delegation and/or significant partner consultation and that is one of the reasons partners are attracted to the firm (compared, say, to working in a larger firm where there is a lesser level of partner consultation and management has considerable authority).

Authority delegated to negotiating team

While there may be perceived valid reasons for partners wishing to have significant and regular consultation on every aspect of the merger negotiations and in effect give the negotiating team relatively little discretion and authority, experience indicates that such an approach tends to be ineffective and does not work well in practice.

Progress is slow because of the need to report back constantly and seek instruction and the process risks degenerating to a situation where in effect the full partnership becomes the negotiating team in every respect except actually sitting round the table. Of course, as indicated previously, there may be certain absolute non-negotiables and it is important that the negotiating team is aware of these from the outset rather than these being 'imposed' mid-way through the discussions. Clearly, however, as with all negotiations, the more extensive the list of non-negotiables and the greater the restrictions on those negotiating the less likely an agreement will be reached (except of course if the other party wants or needs to merge essen-tially 'at any price').

There must always be a concern that if the negotiating team does have very significant limitations placed on it that this is a reflection of, consciously or subconsciously, a preference of some partners not to merge. It could be, for any number of reasons, that such partners do not wish to openly oppose merger and they may perhaps even be perceived to actively support it but then effectively prevent it from occurring by insisting on certain conditions that in essence create impossible barriers.

If there is a suspicion that such circumstances are occurring, it is important that the underlying concerns over merger (or the merger negotiations) are dealt with first rather than entering into merger discussions with unrealistic constraints on the negotiating team.

Ultimately the discretion and authority given to the negotiating team and the level of consultation deemed appropriate is an issue for each partnership to decide on taking into account the circumstances of the situation and critical factors such as:

- the strength of the business case;
- the level of the need to merge;
- the current position and competitiveness of the firm and the implications of merger not occurring;
- the current position and competitiveness of the identified merger partner and the implications for them of merger not occurring;
- the relative attractiveness of the preferred merger partner compared to the second preferred choice.

While all these issues are important, in essence it comes down to a large extent to a single factor, namely just how much the partnership feels it wants (or needs) to merge with the identified preferred partner. Overall, however, the fundamental principle is to give the negotiating team as broad and unconstrained remit as possible (and then ideally add to it!). The team will be acutely aware that they ultimately have to persuade their partners that what they have negotiated is in the partnership's overall best interests and in this context the greater the flexibility and discretion they are given the higher the likelihood that they will be able to identify a win-win agreement; the more constrained they are the more likely that negotiations will become more akin to horse trading rather than a co-operative and constructive process with both parties focused primarily on seeking to find an agreement which is acceptable to each of the legacy partnerships but maximises the competitiveness and likelihood of success of the new firm.

Conducting the merger negotiations: initial meeting

It is impossible to be prescriptive about the structure that merger discussions should follow and circumstance will tend to dictate the order and in what way they should progress.

At the outset, however, it is good practice to have a preliminary scoping meeting agreeing on key issues such as:

- scope of work and work planning;
- intended timing both for negotiations and the preferred effective date of merger;
- tasks to be undertaken by the negotiating team and tasks to be delegated;
- appointment of external advisers – both shared and own party;
- communication – external and internal;
- undertaking of due diligence;
- responsibilities for costs;
- non-poaching agreement should merger not proceed – covering clients, partners, other staff;
- confidentiality undertakings.

Master work plan

Based on this meeting a masterplan for the merger negotiations can be drawn up with clear target dates by which time specific tasks should be completed. These targets, should of course not be considered as inviolable although it has to be recognised that without such a timetable the negotiations are very likely to extend over a longer and longer time period with both enthusiasm and momentum tending to dwindle.

The masterplan should indicate what activities can and could be undertaken consecutively and which have to be undertaken successively with the outcome of one impacting on the decision making of others.

In developing the masterplan it is generally best to ensure that all the likely meetings are at least provisionally scheduled from the outset rather than trying to schedule the next meeting at the conclusion of each meeting; this latter practice inevitably results in delays occurring if the people involved have other significant commitments, client or otherwise.

An example of the key areas of the master work plan is included in Appendix VII.

Timing considerations

There are no hard and fast rules concerning how quickly negotiations should proceed.

Some mergers (although perhaps fairly these tend to be more like take-overs) are known to have been completed in as little as a weekend of working.

Other merger discussions last over a 1–2 month period with $1/_2$–1 day meetings occurring on a weekly basis with preparatory work, partner consultation and so on taking place between these regular meetings.

In other cases the merger discussions last a considerably longer period of time and this can be for a variety of reasons, sometimes planned, sometimes a consequence of factors that arise during the discussions and sometimes a consequence of extraneous, unrelated factors.

There may, for example, be absolutely no urgency to complete the merger discussions or the merger discussions may progress relatively slowly because the agreed effective date for the merger is significantly in the future. Alternatively merger discussions may progress slowly because the two firms want and need time to get to know one another well enough to feel comfortable merging. Or there could be extreme pressure on the time of some or all of those involved in the negotiations, limiting the time they can dedicate to the discussions; or the issues to be resolved may be extremely complex and take time to work through.

As a general principle, however, we would argue for merger negotiations to be undertaken at a relatively rapid rate (say within a 6–12 week period), ideally building both momentum and enthusiasm as they progress.

Achieving this does require both parties to commit to a number of meetings at the outset which can, of course, be cancelled if not required. Based on this schedule, programmes of consultation meetings within each firm can be planned and while the style and approach of these may differ between the firms it is highly likely to be advantageous to keep the programmes in synch across the two partnerships.

Inevitably it is not usually possible to determine the time of year of negotiations but factors such as the potential disruptions of summer holidays and Christmas/New Year breaks need to be considered and the possible distraction of the financial year end billings and collections etc. may also need to be factored in.

Time for launch preparation

An additional consideration is also the timing between the completion of negotiations and the effective date of operation as a merged firm.

In cases where one firm is essentially being absorbed into the other, adopting its systems, identity, structure, partnership deed and so on, there may not need to be a significant period between the completion of negotiations and the 'launch' of the new firm because relatively limited planning or change is required.

In other circumstances a period of several months may be required to allow sufficient time for all the preparatory work required and this is likely to be the case if the two legacy firms have substantially differing systems, either or both front- or back-office, and there is a need to bring these together or migrate to a single new system prior to merger taking effect.

The time to develop a new corporate identity and launch this also requires consideration.

In practice the preparatory work on much of this can commence before the merger negotiations are completed although there is obviously a risk in this and, at the very least, cost implications should the merger ultimately not occur.

Sometimes, however, there is really little option but to at the least commission the initial concept work on a new corporate identity (because of the time required to undertake such a task) prior to the merger negotiations being completed. (And, of course, the judicious 'unveiling' of the proposed new corporate identity can be a very useful step in maintaining enthusiasm in the process and also often acts as a 'tangible' reminder that the merger is 'for real').

At its most basic a new corporate identity will need to be developed and applied to letterheads, business cards and signage and there is also likely to be a need for a new website and brochures although a significant amount of these latter two items may be, at least initially, simple rebadging of existing material from one or both legacy firms.

All this is likely to take, at a minimum, 4 weeks to complete and may require substantially more time.

To prevent cyber-squatting or other parties otherwise registering the proposed new name, it will be important to register possible names as soon as possible as domain names and also as service/trade marks and company names.

Obviously such registrations do have the potential to alert outsiders, including both clients and competitors of the intention to merger (or at least the likelihood of this) and this needs to be considered. In most cases, however, by the point names and so on are being considered, the intention to merger is known to clients and so this is not usually an issue.

Communication

There are two aspects to communication: internal and external and these are separately considered below. An overall general checklist on communications is included as Appendix VIII.

Internal communication during negotiations

The level of communication that it is appropriate to have within a firm during merger negotiations will vary from firm to firm and even then from circumstance to circumstance.

Key factors in particular include the relative scale of the merger, the likely impact it will have on partners – both as owners and in their role as lawyers and possibly managers – and the level of trust and confidence in those leading the merger negotiations. Also, inevitably, the degree to which the merger will create the need for other changes (e.g. capital structure, drawings policy, management and organisation, and so on) will likely impact on the level of communication required.

It is important that the communication is genuinely two-way where that is required with the negotiating team reporting on progress and taking on board feedback from the wider partnership on issues of concern. To achieve such two-way communication, presentations and meetings rather than written reports are likely to be the most appropriate approach.

In other circumstances, periodic reports circulated from the negotiating team will suffice and this is most likely to be the only viable option in larger firms where in any case there may be an acceptance of a lower level of consultation so this form of one-way communication will be the norm.

It is normally good practice for copies of any communication from one firm's negotiating team to their partners to be copied to the other firm's negotiating team although there may be circumstances where this is not appropriate. The copying of such communications helps ensure that there is consistency across the firms and this is important.

The levels to which communication cascades downwards is also a key consideration. Clearly it is important that partners do not discover that their firm is in merger negotiations through the press or through the internet. Equally they should not be relying on or even having such sources as their primary sources of information concerning progress. (See Appendix IX for suggestions for dealing with the press prior to formal announcements being made and Appendix X for a list of typical press questions to which responses may be required).

The same, of course, is true of how other lawyers and staff learn about and receive information concerning the proposed merger. In no circumstances is it advisable to be having lawyers and staff relying primarily on third party sources which inevitably will be communicating from a different perspective and placing a different slant on things.

The prospect of merger is likely to be greeted with enthusiasm by some people and concern by others. Inevitably there will be worries over job security, career prospects and change and it is important that such matters are dealt with effectively in an honest and sensitive way.

Clearly non-partner lawyers and staff will tend to be more interested in the impact of the proposed merger at a personal level than with the broader implications; communication needs to be focused accordingly.

Often having those partners involved in the negotiations sitting down and talking with groups of lawyers and staff and especially the more senior ones is an appropriate way of addressing such issues although time pressures on those involved in the negotiations can make this very difficult to achieve.

There is a real risk that without effective communication the 'rumour-mill' will start running in overdrive and quite possibly be fuelled by those of a mischievous nature with no great loyalty to the firm. Such rumours can be hugely damaging and distracting and impact adversely on motivation, morale and productivity. Furthermore the time, effort and resource to correct such mis-information are always far greater than would have been required to manage a flow of accurate information from the outset.

Furthermore it is important to be aware that both headhunters and recruiters as well as competitors are likely to try and take advantage of any 'instability' created through the uncertainty of a possible merger. Inadequate communication can and does act as a catalyst for those perhaps considering a career move and will certainly be seized on opportunistically by those outside the firm as a good time to increase their efforts to attract good lawyers and support staff.

The communication to non-partners and support staff does not necessarily have to be frequent nor does it have to go into great detail. It should, however, be such that it does provide all or as much as possible of the information as people want and be honest. Empty platitudes of 'everything will stay the same and there will be no change' will not be believed and will result in a loss of confidence if people have reason to believe that this, manifestly, will not be the case.

In the main, short presentations followed by question and answer sessions where people feel able and encouraged to ask about whatever issues are concerning them tend to work best. And the opportunity for one-on-one confidential sessions may also be required.

In larger firms in particular it may be appropriate to set up mechanisms whereby questions and concerns can be posted (possibly on a non-attributable basis) on an electronic 'notice-board' with some form of commitment from the firm concerning the timing of responses to these.

A final point worth making concerns how much detailed information on progress should be made available.

As a general rule it tends to be best to keep this to a minimum because often some of the issues initially agreed upon do have to be revisited later in the negotiations in order to develop mutually acceptable 'solutions' to other issues. For example, certain aspects of the structure and detail of a partner profit-sharing scheme may have to be modified in the light, say, of finalised budgeting for the new firm.

If the original proposals had been communicated it can be very difficult to go back to a partnership and announce that a different approach will after all be required. Better also to present a relatively complete proposed agreement, covering all substantive issues in one package which can be assessed in totality rather than each aspect being considered in isolation and without full context. Apart from anything, certain less palatable aspects may be regarded as more acceptable if considered in the context of other, more 'favourable' aspects of the agreement.

Piecemeal communication of progress tends to serve little purpose and hinders an holistic appraisal being made.

Client communication

Clients are unlikely to want to know the detail of the negotiations but are likely to respond positively to being informed of the possibility of a merger directly from a partner in the firm, rather than by reports in the press, they may also appreciate it if their views on the proposed merger are sought. (We return to this point in the part on client due diligence).

Clients' greatest concern both during merger negotiations and post-merger is that partners and other lawyers will take their 'eyes off the ball' and be distracted by the merger from providing high levels of service. If clients have explained to them the rationale for the merger and have confidence in this and also experience no diminution or dilution in attention or service there is no reason for them to be concerned.

Again, however, merger may be seized on by competitors as an opportunity to try and prise away clients and it is important to guard against this.

Also there may be some clients for whom the possibility of merger acts as a catalyst for reconsidering their choice of legal providers;

possibly because they had already had some concerns over the level and value of service being provided.

It is possible in such circumstances that the prospect of merger will precipitate such a move but the likelihood is that this would have happened irrespective of the possibility of merger and the greater strengths of the merged firm may provide a persuasive argument for such a client or clients to remain with the firm for at least a trial period although clearly they remain 'at risk'.

Press communication

At some point, formal communication with the press concerning the proposed merger will be required. In some circumstances the two firms will decide to manage this process internally and in other circumstances external PR advisers will be appointed. Circumstances will dictate how PR should be managed; an information checklist is included as Appendix XI. (See also Appendix X).

Conducting the negotiations

There is no single, one size fits all, approach to merger negotiations that will suit all circumstances.

Generally, however, it is best to address the most significant issues first and the less significant ones afterwards. And the most significant issues are likely to have been identified during the initial discussions that preceded the actual negotiations. These will vary from case to case but the most common issues tend to be:

- management and organisation structure including agreement on who will fill the key positions during the initial period post-merger and procedures for subsequent election/selection;
- the partnership structure;
- the rights, responsibilities, accountability and expectations of partners; the establishment or otherwise of partner performance appraisals;
- profit sharing approach including the role, authority and responsibility of any remuneration committee assuming a performance related approach is to apply; drawings policy;

- future ownership of any partnership assets owned by either legacy firms including any ancillary businesses;
- capital requirements and funding of this, including policy on internal (partner) versus external (borrowings) funding.

More than, in perhaps, any other type of negotiation there should be an overriding priority on finding win–win positions on all substantive matters that, as stated previously, will maximise the competitiveness of the to be created firm. There may have to be compromise on some points and trade-offs on others; this is perfectly acceptable as long as such compromises and trade-offs are all based on achieving the maximum competitiveness for the new firm.

On some issues one firm's approach may be accepted as the most appropriate and on other issues the other firm's approach may be seen as best. There should, however, on each point not be any aim to impose one or other firm's approach on the new firm but to find the best approach; and this, in many cases, may be the development of a new approach that is based on neither legacy firm's approach.

Developing win-win solutions is not always easy and here perhaps as much as at any point in the merger process outside, expert independent advisers can contribute significantly. Not only will they have the advantage of being 'emotionally' uninvolved but should also bring a wealth of experience from previous work. Above all however, the best such advisers should bring genuine creativity to the negotiations, thinking differently – laterally – to develop 'solutions' to what may seem to those closely involved as intractable issues.

Management issues

An issue that can often create difficulties is a concern within one partnership that it is being taken-over by the other firm and in reality this may or may not be the case.

Interestingly in the world of corporate M&A the markets tend to favour takeover where it is clear that one party or the other is the dominant organisation. There is a sense that in such circumstances strong management will be active from the outset (potentially including senior executives from both legacy organisations) and that the potential benefits of merger will be realised more rapidly.

Shareholders will tend not to be so bothered in the distinction as to whether or not a take-over or merger has occurred – they quite understandably are primarily concerned with accelerated earnings growth and/or increased market value.

Hence the issue of whether a merger or take-over has occurred tends to be more of an issue for the senior management of each organisation.

In law firm mergers the issue is more sensitive and more far reaching.

Those involved in management are naturally concerned. From the point of view of both their partners and the firm's clients they will be concerned about perceptions that their firm has been taken-over and such a take-over is a sign of failure: they may also have concerns over the disappearance of a name, brand and indeed firm with a long and respected history and heritage.

From an 'emotional perspective' such issues are indeed important and of course it would not make any sense to lose the goodwill or 'equity' attached to a firm and its name.

It is important, however, to recognise that such goodwill and equity essentially reside in the people and in particular partners of the firm and, as such, can be effectively and relatively easily transferred to a new firm (possibly requiring certain transitional arrangements to be put in place to facilitate this).

The reality is that clients will not simply transfer their business elsewhere just because of a change in name providing the levels of service that they were previously receiving and were satisfied with are at least maintained in the merged firm and that there are no adverse reputational issues associated with the new firm.

As an important aside it is worth recognising, related to this last point that the converse also applies: namely a merger and change in name will not automatically result in new inflows of work from clients that had previously not been satisfied with the levels of service provided. Nor will new clients who 'test' the new firm remain if their initial experiences result in them being not satisfied with the levels of service provided.

Obvious points perhaps but nevertheless worth making because in many circumstances there do appear to be somewhat unrealistic expectations on these counts with a hope that merger itself, possibly linked with a change in name will deliver significant benefits and act as a panacea for any weaknesses or shortcomings in one or both parties to the merger.

Of course one of the firms in the merger negotiations may be in a weaker position with less strong economics or partners or client base or practice area strengths (or some combination of these) than it would prefer compared to the other firm. But there have to be certain significant strengths or potential in such a firm for the other firm to be considering merger so 'failure' hardly seems an appropriate description although it can become, unfortunately, embedded in the thinking and result in firms not being as open-minded as they might be in conducting merger negotiations (and of course in the preceding stages leading to the identification of potential merger partners).

From a more personal perspective those in management positions in the 'smaller firm' (or firm being taken over) are highly likely to have individual concerns.

Some may relish the opportunity of giving up their management roles and responsibilities and return full time to client facing work. Others may be relatively sanguine about the implications: more than willing to continue with management responsibilities, albeit most likely in a different role or with differing responsibilities in the merged firm if they are considered the most appropriate and best suited to fulfil such positions. Others may be disappointed at the loss of a management role but accept this as a 'cost' of merger and/or recognise that in due course there may be opportunities to become involved in management again.

There are, however, circumstances where the lack of a management role for one or more partners is a very significant issue personally and/or professionally. From a personal view there can be immense disappointment and also a blow to their ego that they are not considered most suited to fulfil a position in management (or, at least, the position they cherish). The implications can be even more far reaching if such partners do not wish to or cannot for some reason return to a client facing role.

For such partners merger can represent a watershed in their careers and it is critical that the firm as a whole addresses such issues sensitively but commercially and in keeping with their culture and values. To do otherwise risks the merger negotiations failing to reach a satisfactory conclusion as there is a very real likelihood that 'conflict' will emerge between the positions of certain individuals and the partnership as a whole.

Clearly there may be some space for flexibility here but this must not be allowed to reach proportions whereby the future competitiveness of the merged firm becomes compromised.

The underlying principle needs to be one of the most appropriate person filling each position and should they largely or exclusively come from one firm so be it, subject to this not being entirely demotivating to partners in the other firm.

Finding or creating management positions for certain people, essentially as a 'sop' to them or to try and demonstrate to the market, the press and clients that it is not a take-over is, usually, a poor long term strategy to follow although as indicated there may be reasons to do this in the short term.

Law firm merger negotiations have historically broken down and no doubt will continue to break down in the future over the issues of who will fulfil key management and leadership roles. Some such breakdowns are perhaps in the best long term interests of the firms involved because, in reality, they are based on issues of which firm's management approach will prevail in the new firm and possibly there is a genuine incompatibility here. In other cases it is essentially to do with personal egos and related to this concerns over perceptions of one firm being taken over by or subsumed in the other.

In such circumstances it can only be concluded as a travesty if merger supported by an overwhelming business rationale does not take place because of concerns or irreconcilable differences over such issues.

Furthermore there is a certain irony in all of this because, a priori, it is generally exceptionally difficult to identify which particular person is best suited to fulfil a certain role in the new firm. This is especially the case if say both such 'candidates' have fulfilled similar roles in the legacy firms to a broadly similar degree of success.

Even if such circumstances do not exist, it has to be recognised that in an enlarged firm very different characteristics and capabilities may be required of the leadership and management team members than those required in the legacy firms. And although it is perhaps unlikely, it is not inconceivable that a partner who may not have fulfilled a management role in one of the legacy firms will be the ideal person to fulfil a large role, in the combined firm.

Three key issues

Aside from these particular personality driven issues (i.e. who will fulfil which role) three issues on which merger discussions tend to falter concern the overall management structure, the role and expectations of partners and partner remuneration.

These are addressed below.

Management structure

Over the years a very considerable body of principles concerning management structure in law firms has been developed. As with any principles they can of course be disregarded and/or broken but better by far that this be undertaken knowingly rather than unwittingly.

Outlining the theory and principles of effective management structures for law firms is beyond the scope of this book and, would constitute an entire book in its own right. There are, however, a number of overriding considerations of management structures and seven of these are listed below:

(i)   The structure must provide a means for taking both strategic and operational decisions;

(ii) There must be clear definitions of roles, responsibilities, accountabilities and lines of communication throughout the structure;

(iii) The structure requires a central function able to co-ordinate and 'direct' resources/activities so that they are aligned with the firm's strategic objectives and goals;

(iv) Operational decisions should be taken by those who are responsible for implementing them and taken as close to the point of action as possible;

(v)   Business Units should seek to make decisions that are in the best interests of the firm;

(vi) Partners must be prepared to work within the delegated responsibilities that they (as owners) have given to management;

(vii) The decision-making process must be effective, efficient, and a source of cohesion for the partnership.

Developing a new management and organisation structure should certainly take note of these principles and if disregarding any of them, do so knowingly and with forethought of the implications.

Ultimately the design of the merged firm's management and organisation structure should be driven primarily from the perspective of the agreed objectives and strategy, taking into account factors such as the size and geographic coverage of the combined firm.

There is, however, a real danger that either through lack of knowledge or through an unwillingness to confront difficult issues, that an inappropriate management and organisation structure is agreed. At the very least this is likely to compromise the ability of the merged firm to operate effectively and realise the opportunities identified and at worst it may jeopardise the entire merger.

Typical shortcomings that can emerge include:

- unclear roles, responsibilities and levels of authority in key management positions;
- unclear accountabilities, both for partners in general and those in key management positions;
- a plethora of joint responsibilities for key management roles (e.g. joint managing partners) although in exceptional circumstances this can work effectively;
- one or more disconnects in reporting lines and responsibilities between partners (or more accurately the partnership) as owners of the business and partners as operating lawyers (i.e. the link between the partnership : management : offices : practice groups : partners);
- unclear primary and secondary lines of responsibility, authority and accountability in matrix based structures;
- 'fudging' on certain key positions to work around difficult (sometimes prima donna personality type) partners;
- the implementation of a structure that fails to facilitate rapid integration of the strengths of each partnership and/or is not aligned with key aims of the merged firm (i.e. managing primarily along office lines when the aim is to develop clients on a national (or international) basis).

In developing a new management and organisational structure there are particular advantages in seeking external expertise; experienced external advisers can help ensure that the new structure:

(i) is aligned with and supportive of the achievement of the merged firm's strategic objectives;

(ii) recognises the approach each legacy firm has previously followed and is sensitive to and realistic concerning the changes required to migrate to the new structure and ensure it operates effectively;

(iii) meets the principles of effective management and organisational structures or, if not, is aware of this and the likely implications.

In respect of all of the above a significant role for any external advisers will be in ensuring all partners, both those with management positions and those without, are properly informed about how the management and organisational structure will operate in practice and the implications for and impact on individuals.

This is likely to be particularly important if the new structure does include significant change in areas such as:

(i) the role, responsibility and authority vested in key management groups and individuals;

(ii) the levels of consultation and involvement of partners in decision making;

(iii) the performance and contribution expectations of partners and/or their levels of autonomy (see following section where this point is elaborated).

In addition external advisers can assist in the process of helping select the most appropriate partners to fill the key management positions.

Whether undertaken in a very formal way or more informally, external advisers can assist in ensuring that there is genuine clarity concerning the expectations of each of the key management positions and boards and that the best suited people are selected accordingly.

In particular external consultants can be very helpful in removing some of the 'parochialism' that tends to emerge and help defuse the emotions surrounding the selection for particular roles.

Consultants can also help ensure that management boards and committees are constituted of partners with a suitably diverse and mixed set of characteristics and capabilities although not to the point where they would be unable to operate effectively as a group.

Role and expectations of partners

In theory it could be argued that the role and expectations of partners is not a negotiation issue in as much as the topic need not be addressed directly in either the merger agreement nor except in fairly general terms in the merged firm's partnership deed.

This, however, badly misses the point.

Based on the strategic aims of the combined firm there will be a series of objectives and levels of performance that will need to be achieved.

Some such objectives and performance levels will be in economic terms and concern hours (both chargeable and non-chargeable), expected leverage, billings, collections, WIP, AR and so on. Clearly it is critical that the 'sum' of the expected contributions/performance levels of partners does result in a level of firm performance consistent with the achievement of the firm's strategic and financial objectives.

Equally importantly each partner needs to understand and commit to such levels of performance and contribution. And it is for this reason as much as any other that the performance and contribution expectations of partners need to be established early on and clearly.

Such performance and contribution expectations should not, however, be seen purely in terms of financial performance as this will tend to result in an overly narrow focus.

Furthermore it may transpire that in financial terms only limited changes in performance expectations are expected.

The more significant changes, more likely than not, will concern the expectations of partners outside of their client facing, fee generating work. Clearly in this respect the expectations will be very much circumstance dependent.

Nevertheless behind many mergers is an objective to improve the quality and/or volume of clients and instructions; in parallel there is often an aim of increasing the levels of cross-selling achieved. Often also, and frequently associated with the above, is an aim of institutionalising more client relationships which, in turn, requires a shift from a 'my client' to 'the firm's client' mindset.

Achieving such shifts, which can impact in a fundamental way on the day to day priorities and behaviours of partners, is a very major challenge as it goes to the very core of what the role of a partner is: their working day raison d'être.

Failing to ensure high levels of understanding on this throughout both partnerships is likely to be a fatal weakness in the merged firm. And, equally important, of course, is building high levels of commitment to achieving such change.

Hence it is vitally important as part of the merger discussions that there is a properly focused discussion and agreement on the role and expectations of partners and while it would be inappropriate to be prescriptive on this point, it is generally worth including in the merger documentation some detail on this issue and also ensure that it is discussed and widely understood through the consultation process.

A lack of understanding by partners of the required changes and/ or a lack of commitment to making the required changes will undermine the fundamental rationale to merge.

Partner remuneration

Bringing together two firms with significantly different approaches to profit sharing can be difficult and this is particularly the case if the underlying reason for the differing approaches is a reflection of fundamentally differing philosophies or values: for example one is focused on individual performance while the other more on team performance or one is lockstep and the other merit based.

And, of course, significant difference in the ratios between the least and most highly remunerated partners can cause additional challenges.

Factors such as whether the mechanisms and indeed even the outputs of the profit sharing approaches are transparent or not are important factors, as are differences in whether the schemes both work the same or differently in terms of a prospective or retrospective basis of allocating points. (Only relevant for performance-based schemes).

There may also be complexities created by the two firms operating in differing geographic markets that will each bear differing levels of fees and the impact of this on profit. Such differences can also occur if the two firms have differing practice strengths each commanding somewhat different levels of fees.

On top there may of course be significant differences in the absolute levels of profitability of the two firms and such differences may be either productivity (fees per fee earner and partner) or cost (salaries and overheads) driven or some combination of the two.

This too can add complexity to the task of developing and agreeing an appropriate approach to partner profit sharing.

In a buoyant market where the outlook for profit growth based on increasing levels of client demand is strong, there tends to be more flexibility to find 'solutions'. Equally if the proposed merger is likely to result in significant cost savings, say the combination of the two firms into single premises with no ongoing property liabilities, then again developing an appropriate structure for moving forward can be that little bit easier.

In reality, however, such circumstances, while highly welcome, are not present in most mergers.

Again this is an issue where it is not possible to be pragmatic on how an appropriate new scheme for the combined firm should be developed, although as an underlying principle it is important to start as far as is possible with a clean sheet of paper and an open mind and develop an approach that is best suited to the needs of the combined new firm rather than an imposition or adaptation of either legacy firm's approach.

It is almost always best to address this issue in two stages: first to develop and agree the basic philosophy and approach that should underpin the profit sharing:

- lockstep, modified lockstep or performance;
- ratio (or limits) between lowest and highest profit shares;
- length of lockstep in years if appropriate;
- transparent or non-transparent operation/output;
- prospective or retrospective operation;
- if performance or part performance-based, criteria to be used, if any, in assessing contribution.

Once this has been agreed in principle the second stage can be undertaken and this involves evaluating the proposed approach and establishing the 'results' it would produce under various different levels of profit and performance.

Pragmatism has to play a major part here and a degree of 'tweaking' may be required or possibly even a more fundamental rethink if the output of the modelling appears inappropriate.

Underlying all of this will be a need, assuming the two firms are moving to a single profit pool, of placing the partners of the two firms fairly on a single points 'ladder' irrespective of whether it is lockstep or performance based.

To achieve this it is important to ascertain whether partners from the two firms at a similar position on their respective firm's profit sharing are indeed making a similar level of contribution and the output to such analysis may necessitate a certain degree of 'shuffling'.

One approach here can be to analyse the two firms' recent profitability, trends in these and future profit forecasts; on the basis of this an initial allocation of profit proportions between the two legacy firms can be made. Each partnership can then allocate their proportion to their partners to form a basis of profit shares for Year 1 with the combined firm's agreed approach coming into play thereafter.

Such an approach is by no means appropriate in all circumstances but it does get round the difficulty of neither firm knowing as much as they might prefer about the levels of performance and contribution of the other firm's partners prior to merger.

As a final point here it is clearly vital that the approach adopted is consistent with and supportive/encouraging of the behaviour expected within the new firm. If, for example, client sharing or a focus on team based new business development is required by the merged firm this is not likely to be achieved if the profit sharing approach does or is perceived to recognise and reward primarily other factors, say individual partner billings.

On this point it is important to recognise that if in either or both firms there is some nervousness or anxiety about the merger there is likely to be a certain heightened level of inherent 'my client syndrome'. Understandably partners will regard their clients as both a potential safety parachute and 'golden key' providing the entry to a new practice should they decide to move.

Probably no remuneration scheme will have a hugely significant impact in changing such concerns and resulting behaviour but it should, most certainly not encourage it and in the immediate post-merger period and possibly beyond, the value of opening up client relationships and providing both a broader and deeper range of services should be encouraged and recognised in every way possible.

Due diligence

Due diligence is likely to cover a wide range of areas some of which are relatively defined in scope, such as professional indemnity cover and claims record, premises, other financial liabilities, and so on while others are potentially much more extensive in scope covering financial and accounting matters, client satisfaction and loyalty, partner and possibly senior associate commitment, and so on.

Clearly the output of any aspect of the due diligence may result in one or other party deciding they do not wish to proceed with the merger or have certain changes to the merger agreement incorporated (e.g. ring-fencing of particular liabilities or assets).

It should be made clear, however, that full and frank disclosure should have occurred prior to any due diligence taking place and so there should be minimal change to the merger agreement as a consequence of the due diligence if the previous exchange of information and related analyses have been undertaken effectively.

What can emerge as a consequence of the due diligence is a recognition that certain information that has been exchanged is not on a strictly like-for-like basis (e.g. valuation of WIP or other accounting treatments) or that certain information that has been exchanged has not been properly understood.

In such circumstances some amendments to the merger agreement are likely to need to be considered.

Equally importantly the role of the due diligence is to manage expectations – to ensure each party to the merger is fully aware of the circumstances of the other firm.

There are two approaches to any due diligence that can be considered:

1. for each firm to undertake due diligence by appointing its own advisers to review those aspects of the other firm as it sees fit;
2. for the two firms jointly to appoint the same advisers to undertake the same due diligence on each firm.

Of course some combination of the two approaches can also be considered with certain aspects of the due diligence undertaken under the first option and other aspects under the second.

Accounting and financial due diligence

The accounting and financial due diligence is invariably undertaken by accountants, either the existing accountants of each firm undertaking the due diligence on the other firm or one or both parties appointing new accountants specifically for this task. (Incidentally this can provide a useful opportunity to 'test' new accountants as potential advisers for the merged firm in the future).

From a 'conflict' perspective there is no professional reason why one firm of accountants should not undertake the due diligence on both firms and this situation can arise because each firm previously has used the same accountants or because both firms agree to use the same accountants for this specific task.

If both firms decide to use the same accountants for the due diligence it tends to be best to appoint accountants who have previously either acted for both firms or neither firm.

Having joint accountants undertaking the due diligence who have previously had a working relationship with one firm but not the other can be regarded as unsatisfactory or unacceptable although can work well.

The exact scope of the financial due diligence will depend on circumstances and it is important that the firms or firm involved be clearly briefed.

In this respect it is also important to recognise that relatively few firms of accountants have significant experience in undertaking due diligence on law firms and if this is an important consideration it will influence the selection of firm.

Firms of accountants without significant experience with law firms may also have greater difficulty in reconciling the different accounting approaches used by the two firms and this is particularly likely to be the case if one of the approaches is unfamiliar to them.

Typically the financial and accounting due diligence will cover some or all of the following areas:

1. Accounts and accounting policies – balance sheet / profit and loss;
2. Intangible assets, debtors and work in progress;

3. Cash flow forecasts;
4. Compliance with appropriate bar rules;
5. Pension Fund – description of pension arrangements in operation;
6. Partners: movement in the number of partners and performance;
7. Impact on fees of known partners' retirement/partners giving notice;
8. Associates considered for promotion to partner;
9. Tax.

Typically this due diligence will require 2–3 weeks to complete but this will be largely dependent on the agreed scope, the size of the firms involved, the adequacy or otherwise of their financial records, the availability or otherwise of key members of the finance department to provide data, address issues and so on.

Consideration should also be given concerning the type and style of reporting that would be most helpful and this is something that is best discussed both at the outset and again just prior to reports being drafted.

In this context it is also worth considering whether one or more reports are required as it may be appropriate to produce a more 'technically' oriented report for those specifically involved in or with responsibility for financial and accounting matters and a more 'general' report for wider circulation. (In this respect the 'technical' report may also focus, if this is within the agreed brief, on integration issues, structuring of the merger to minimise tax liabilities, and so on).

In planning and undertaking the financial due diligence the checklist for financial integration included in Appendix XII may be of value.

Client due diligence

Client due diligence is often seen as not strictly necessary and the argument put forward tends to be based on the fact that each firm has longstanding relationships with its key clients and that the fee income from these clients has shown growth over the years; hence, the argument goes, the client must be satisfied with the services provided so why undertake due diligence?

There is, of course, a degree of validity in this argument but this does not mean that considerable value will not emerge from undertaking due diligence.

Circumstances will again dictate the scope and focus of the due diligence but in general such exercises tend to focus on:

(i)   current levels of satisfaction and loyalty of key clients of each firm;
(ii) such clients' reaction to the proposed merger;
(iii) opportunities created by the proposed merger to broaden or deepen the range of services provided.

Generally speaking it is best if such due diligence is undertaken by a single external organisation interviewing a similar number of clients of each firm, undertaking each interview in a consistent fashion. If each firm appoints its own advisers to undertake the interviews there will be no certainty of consistency or comparability of results and this significantly devalues the worth of the exercise.

As an alternative each firm can interview a small number of the other firm's key clients itself but there are a number of weaknesses in this approach including a lack of consistency and also the unlikelihood of either firm having suitably trained and experienced people capable of undertaking such a task. Furthermore all the experience indicates that fuller, franker and richer feedback is obtained from interviews if they are undertaken by independent, experienced external specialists.

Face to face interviews do tend to provide the best information for such due diligence but given the relatively narrow focus of these interviews (and often significant timing constraints) it often becomes necessary to undertake some, if not all, of the interviews over the 'phone.

Typically no more than 10–15 interviews of clients of each firm may be undertaken and while this is a small sample size a programme of this scope can nevertheless provide very valuable information particularly if it is focused exclusively on the largest clients of each firm (typically the largest 10 clients of a firm can account for c.20% upwards of the total income of that firm).

As well as such interviews providing valuable information on the prime issues designed to be addressed, other substantial benefits are also likely to arise:

(i) clients will tend to feel pleased that their views have been sought;

(ii) the exercise will also be seen as a tangible demonstration of each firm's commitment to its key clients and their concerns;

(iii) any underlying client concerns over service will be identified and can be addressed (irrespective of whether the merger proceeds);

(iv) the output of such an exercise is of tremendous value post-merger in planning and implementing initiatives to improve and widen/deepen the range of services offered to key clients.

Undertaking client due diligence is neither a lengthy nor expensive exercise and its value is very considerable. It remains, however, something which is not always considered and while there are certain circumstances where it is not appropriate to undertake, there are undoubtedly many more circumstances where client due diligence should have been undertaken: in some circumstances it would have been highly likely to have indicated that mergers that ultimately proved unsuccessful should not have even taken place and in other circumstances would have contributed significantly to the post-merger integration process and more effective realisation of the potential benefits of merger.

Partner due diligence

The two major assets of a law firm are its clients and its people and in the previous paragraphs we have explored undertaking due diligence on the former; in this part we explore undertaking due diligence on the latter.

A critical concern in any merger is whether any key partners will depart post-merger because they are uncommitted to the merger or discover subsequently that the merged firm is not to their liking.

Clearly in the first stage of the due diligence exercise it is important for each firm to have full career information on the other firm's partners and equally clearly there should be concerns if the career record of key partners indicates regular changes of firm; partners whose career to date indicates regular moves from firm to firm tend to continue with such behaviour.

The second stage of the due diligence here is for senior management of each firm to meet and get to know the key partners from the other firm, asses their capabilities and gauge their commitment to the merger. This is clearly an art not a science but those in senior management positions will tend to have substantial experience of judging partners and their levels of commitment, although ultimately there will be a degree of intuition in any conclusions reached. This is also an area where external advisers may be able to contribute but great sensitivity is obviously required in involving third parties.

The process of partner due diligence tends to be somewhat less structured and formal than either the financial or client due diligence although this is not always the case. Generally it tends to be undertaken through a series of meetings, dinners and lunches and while there may be some form of 'agenda' such get togethers remain relatively informal. In other albeit relatively rare circumstances a more formal approach is pursued that may include psychometric and similar profiling.

Clearly if there is an indication that one or more of the key partners from one or other firm are not fully committed then further steps may need to be taken.

This could involve more direct conversations with particular partners and might even lead to a decision by one firm or the other or both to impose certain lock-in provisions in the merger agreement; such lock-ins might cover all partners or just a subset comprising those considered as business critical.

Formal 'lock-in' provisions raise a range of complex issues and a series of important questions, not least of which is whether there is much point in 'contractually' forcing someone to remain in the merged firm who does not wish to; after all they are hardly likely to be highly motivated or high performing in such circumstances. (An alternative may be to consider less attractive terms in terms of profit shares, withdrawal of capital etc. for those who depart soon after merger but even the 'benefits' of this need to be weighed up very carefully against the drawbacks).

In many mergers worries over partner resignations and fallout are hardly an issue at all but for other mergers it is a significant concern and causes more lost sleep than anything else.

Due diligence on this cannot remove the risk, but can certainly help manage it and ensure that post-merger there is a focus on creating the appropriate internal environment and targeting the right set of clients and work that will encourage the key partners of both firms to be enthusiastic and committed to the merged firm.

Generally speaking it is very unusual for the partner due diligence to result in a firm deciding not to proceed with merger but this is not unknown. As a general rule concerns about 'people' tend to emerge rather earlier in the process with a growing unease from one or other firm about compatibility or levels of genuine commitment/buy in to the merger and the strategic aims of the firm to be created.

Concluding the negotiations

As indicated previously two key documents will normally be required as output to the merger negotiations, namely:

1. A merger agreement specifying how the two partnerships will combine, including details of the bringing together of the respective assets and liabilities. Included in this document will be any warranties, etc., provided and also, if appropriate, details of any transitional arrangements.

   There is no set form to such agreements nor to the scope of their coverage. In some circumstances the terms of the merger agreement may be just a few pages and in other circumstances run to 200 pages or more.

2. A partnership deed for the merged firm indicating the basis on which it will operate, its governance, management and so on.

   The deed may be largely based on the existing deed of one or other of the legacy firms if this is felt to be appropriate or be an entirely new deed, drafted from first principles to suit the circumstances of the new firm.

In addition to these two documents there may be a requirement for a prospectus or information memorandum concerning the proposed merger. This tends to be required when larger firms are involved in merger as an effective way of informing all partners; smaller firms do however find that they too derive considerable benefit from drafting such a prospectus in that it brings together all the relevant information about the merger in one place.

Again there is no set form to such a document but it will tend to include:

- a brief description of each firm;
- a summary of the business case;
- key values and operating policies of the new firm;
- financial arrangements;
- structure of new firm;
- management and governance of the new firm (including details of initial appointees);
- partner matters;
- support infrastructure policies and issues;
  - Accounting and financial
  - IT
  - KM
  - HR
  - Marketing

In practice none of these two (or three) documents may need to be signed by all partners, with drafts being endorsed by each partnership and a small group of partners from each firm being delegated the authority to finalise and sign-off on the completed documents.

Part III
Achieving Post-merger Integration

6
Post-merger Integration

Need for planning

As indicated previously the reality of merger is that it, per se, tends to deliver relatively little.

Bringing together two firms creates a larger firm; it also will create a firm with greater strength in depth in existing practice areas and/or a broader range of service capabilities. It may also have a presence in a greater number of geographic locations and might possibly also have a lower cost base.

All important factors but not usually sufficient to justify merger nor in most cases the primary motivation or rationale for merger.

The major benefits of merger do not emerge directly from the bringing together of two firms but from the opportunities created by the bringing together of two firms and the post-merger integration plan's primary purpose is to establish how such opportunities might be realised.

More specifically the purpose of the plan is to establish how the combined firm will: service existing clients more effectively; target and win new clients of the type desired; develop increased competitiveness; improve margins and profitability; and so on. The plan also needs to establish how a unifying set of values and culture for the merged firm might be developed.

The fundamental aim of the plan is to 'translate' the business rationale behind the merger into a set of clear objectives and a 'roadmap' indicating how such objectives will be realised; this in turn will establish the projects and activities that will need to be undertaken and also the resourcing implications.

Post-merger integration plans tend to have three major aspects although each of these may not necessarily be addressed separately:

(i) first, there is a need to identify those issues that must be addressed by the effective date of merger to enable the merged firm to operate effectively; (in strict terms it can be argued that this aspect is concerned with pre-merger integration);

(ii) secondly, there is a need to identify those issues that need to be addressed post-merger in order for the merged firm to realise its aims; typically these issues might be identified in terms of those to be addressed in each of the first 3 months, 6 months, 1 year and 3 years;

(iii) thirdly, there is a need to establish how a set of values and appropriate culture for the merged firm might be developed in a managed way rather than simply allowing 'nature to take its course'.

As with many other types of plan, as much value tends to be derived from the planning process as the plan itself.

In the context of post-merger integration planning the value is generated through focusing on achieving a high level of integration and leverage of the merged firm's capabilities that result in a level of competitiveness that goes far beyond a basic combination of the two legacy firms. This requires those involved in the planning process to consider two sets of issues in particular:

(i) first, there is a need to consider the key steps in building and exploiting the capabilities and enhanced competitiveness of the merged firm in terms of, for example, client management and development, achieving higher levels of performance, and so on;

(ii) secondly, what the barriers to integration are and how they might be removed; in this context issues of the legacy firms' cultures, processes and structures will all be critical.

Benefits of post-merger plan

Over recent years there has been an increasing recognition of the enormous value of developing a post-merger integration plan and

this is at least in part a reflection of the recognition of the requirement for change post-merger if the combined firm is to achieve the
benefits identified. In parallel there has been a recognition that
there is a degree of risk, sometimes substantial, associated with
merger, both financial and reputational, and that the development
of a well thought through post-merger integration plan can play a
major role in managing this risk.

There are in practice such a wide range of benefits that emerge
from producing a post-merger integration plan that it remains surprising that doing this is not a universal occurrence. Five major
advantages include:

(i)   it helps identify and include in a single blueprint everything
      that needs to occur post-merger and included in this can
      be a masterplan of roles, responsibilities and expected timings;
      it provides a clear indication of the degree of change and
      development required;
(ii) it allows realistic budgets to be drawn up establishing the one-
      off and ongoing costs associated with the implementation
      of the plan; as such (even in draft form) it can be an impor-
      tant, and potentially very important, aspect of the decision
      making on whether to merge;
(iii) it allows partners to understand more fully the implications of
      merger, both as owners of the enlarged business and in their
      role as lawyers, and thus make more fully informed decisions as
      to whether to merge or not;
(iv) related to the above it helps ensure that people know what
      they are committing to when they consider merger and so
      post-merger they cannot justifiably argue that they had not
      been made aware of the changes in their role, the way the
      firm would be managed, etc.; in this respect it helps manage
      expectations;
(v)   by involving partners in the development of the post-merger
      integration plan they become more involved in the overall
      merger process and through such involvement a sense of
      ownership and commitment to the combined firm and its
      success starts to be built across a wider cross-section of
      partners.

Pre-merger and launch planning

Prior to the effective launch of a merged firm there are a considerable number of issues that should be addressed. In an ideal world, all of these would be addressed pre-merger but timing issues, financial constraints, other resource considerations or indeed other factors may prevent this occurring. Clearly in such circumstances prioritising and pragmatism have to rule.

Circumstances will dictate the exact range of issues to be addressed pre-merger but the list is likely to include:

- adoption of a new name (including registration of name);
- development and implementation of a new corporate identity;
- development of new marketing material – including website;
- notification to and approval from regulatory and/or statutory bodies;
- accounting conventions, procedures, policies and systems;
- development/integration of systems (IT, billing, practice management, time recording, knowledge management, word processing, document management, telephones, voice messaging, intranet and extranet);
- development of common HR policies (salaries, hours, holiday, pensions, health, disability & life cover, other benefits, performance expectations and management).

In some circumstances the pre-merger planning is relatively clearly defined from the outset with one firm quite simply adopting the name, identity, systems, policies and so on of the other. This is not necessarily indicative of a takeover although could be. Such an adoption of one firm's 'persona' and modus operandi by the other could be equally to do with one firm being more advanced than the other in such respects or when a firm in a particular jurisdiction or location joins another firm that is already operating in a number of jurisdictions or locations and has already in place effective means of operating across jurisdictional boundaries and/or in multiple locations.

In other circumstances there will be a degree of 'trade-off' between the two merging firms: 'We'll adopt your document management system and knowledge management approach if you'll adopt our practice management, time recording and billing systems'. There is not anything necessarily inherently wrong in such trade-offs and it can be argued that the adoption of each others' systems etc. to some extent is both symbolic of the merging of the two firms and their integration and is also a means of sharing the 'pain' of merging: staff in both firms carry some of the burden.

A more strategic approach than this, however, is to take decisions on what approach to adopt on each issue based on maximising the overall competitiveness of the new firm. Overlaying this will of course be financial and other resource considerations in as much as adopting a completely new approach on some issues (i.e. a different approach from that used by either legacy firm) may well be the 'best' approach in terms of maximising competitiveness but from a short-term financial perspective be considered too expensive compared to the next best option or, for example, require such a level of time in, say, retraining of people to be rejected.

On the overriding basis of 'maximising competitiveness' and taking into account timing considerations, the appropriate approach on each issue should be decided and project plans and budgets developed indicating how integration will be achieved.

Circumstances will dictate whether a 'big-bang' or a more evolutionary, gradual integration approach will be most appropriate and if the latter, how 'patches' can be implemented in the meantime to allow the two legacy firms' existing approaches to operate side-by-side over a period of time, perhaps with a level of convergence occurring prior to full integration and the adoption of a single, unified approach at some point in the future.

Given the great number of issues that do need to be addressed and the inherent upheaval and distraction of merger there is a rationale for trying to minimise the range of matters with which partners, lawyers and other staff will have to cope at the outset and this is one strong argument for seeking opportunities, where possible, to develop 'patches' between the two legacy firms' approaches and phase the changes over a period of time.

The counter argument of course is that it is better psychologically and from a business perspective to go for complete merger on Day 1 and get as much as possible of the 'pain of change' over in a short intensive period.

One issue in particular to focus on is the ongoing financial implications of integrating the two legacy firms' HR policies. Clearly here there are a range of employment law considerations in terms of potential changes to terms and conditions of employment. In order to avoid such issues there can be a temptation to adopt the most beneficial or generous (from the employees' perspective) approach of each of the legacy firms on each issue and while this may be regarded very positively by staff, the overall costs can mount quickly and become substantial, particularly if this covers a range of issues such as: salaries, number of days' holiday, core hours, overtime payment, pensions, health cover and other benefits, car allowances, payment for mobile 'phones, provision of home computer equipment etc.

In particular it is important to recognise that these costs are not a one-off but represent increases in ongoing costs that the merged firm will carry indefinitely.

Developing a plan

The starting point for developing a post-merger integration plan is to establish the 'gap' between where the two firms, combined, will be on the effective date of merger and where the merged firm needs to be in, say, each of 1, 2, 3 and 5 years post-merger in order that its strategic objectives are achieved.

In parallel with the strategic objectives there are likely to be certain specific economic objectives, both more immediate and medium-longer term; these may include both top-line, fee income growth targets and also bottom line, profit targets. Either or both sets of targets may be articulated in absolute terms and/or in relative terms compared to peer group competitors.

Achieving these financial targets is clearly very important and this can raise particular challenges if the achievement of these is, in some way, in 'conflict' with the achievement of the strategic objectives. For example the achievement of the former may necessitate some curtailment or slowing down in investment in, say, IT or business development or training and professional development.

The challenge frequently revolves around the issue that people have expectations, often not fully realistic ones, concerning what merger will deliver in terms of improved financial performance in the short term, although the reality is such financial improvements are normally only achieved after a period of investment, both financial and in terms of effort and commitment.

This all argues for caution and conservatism to be taken in terms of financial forecasting and budgeting of the expected performance of the merged firm and in parallel, a management of partner expectations to realistic levels; this is an area where there are substantial benefits of under-promising and overdelivering and not just in financial terms; the adverse impact of achieving the opposite tends to be hugely detrimental.

Clearly the nature of the 'gap' between the current and desired position will determine the scope and focus of the plan. The following list, however, indicates the most commonly included issues to be covered in a post-merger integration plan:

(i)   achieving partner contribution and performance in line with expectations;

(ii)   achieving performance levels throughout the firm consistent with the merged firm's underlying financial and business model;

(iii) establishing appropriate roles, responsibilities, accountabilities and expectations for management – both committees/boards and individuals,

(iv)   achieving practice group integration;

(v)   achieving a one firm style and approach;

(vi)   developing and implementing a unified approach to client relationship management;

(vii) developing and implementing an effective programme of strategically targeted new business development;

(viii) developing and implementing a single, uniform set of HR policies and practices covering recruitment, training and development, appraisals, career progression (including admission to equity).

Each of these topics is explored in the latter part of this chapter. First, however, it is worthwhile commenting on three other issues of critical importance.

Vision, strategy, values and culture

A critical component of success concerns ensuring that the vision and strategy for the merged firm is understood by all staff and that high levels of commitment to their successful achievement are built up and maintained.

It can be argued that this needs to occur pre-merger and this is of course true. The reality, however, is that the understanding of and commitment to the vision and strategy pre-merger is somewhat theoretical or 'in principle'. It obviously needs to be strong enough to commit people to the merger but this clearly is not the same as being committed to pursuing the vision and strategy over what is likely to be the next 5–10 years.

The aim is to develop a vision for the merged firm that is aspirational, credible, motivating and compelling and also to develop a high level of 'buy-in' to this so that all professional and support staff strive to achieve it.

Associated with this, a set of core values for the merged firm need to be developed and these should guide the behaviours that the firm expects of its people – 'the way we do things here'.

During the immediate post-merger period there are inevitably a great number of highly pressing issues to address and there is a tendency to either overlook the 'soft' issues or to see them as of relatively lower importance: these are high risk approaches to follow and the creation and commitment to an integrating vision and set of values is increasingly regarded as a critical factor in the success or otherwise of mergers to deliver the aspired results.

In the immediate post-merger period there is a unique opportunity to influence the values and culture of the firm through establishing an appropriate vision and linked to this a set of behavioural expectations. During this period there is a window of opportunity and while inevitably there will be doubts, concerns and stress during this period there is also optimism and openness: a chance to influence in a substantive way so many aspects of the new firm including the values and culture rather than leaving it to chance and circumstance how they evolve.

If only limited focus is given to the creation of an integrating vision, set of values and culture in the 'honeymoon' period, a key opportunity will have been missed and an inappropriate, possibly non-constructive internal environment can develop and/or a conflict between the values and culture of the two legacy firms can grow and do so in a destructive way.

There are a number of different approaches that can be taken to how to address this issue and there is a great danger in pursuing an inappropriate approach; for example adopting an approach used successfully in another firm or in a previous merger without considering its appropriateness in the specific circumstances.

At best pursuing an inappropriate approach will simply not work; at worst it can alienate and demotivate staff from one or both firms and potentially to a very significant extent.

Developing an integrating vision, set of values and culture tends to be most successfully achieved working at least in part with external advisers who bring objectivity, expertise and experience, none of which are likely to be present within the firm. The complexity of this topic takes it outside the scope of this book although the following general principles are intended to provide an overall framework:

(i) The merged firm's top management needs to be committed to the process – in terms of both their active involvement and 'championing' of the initiative; clear leadership and accountability are a 'must'.

(ii) The top management must behave as role models and be seen to be actively recognising and encouraging behaviour consistent with the initiative and effectively addressing inconsistent and non-supportive behaviours.

(iii) The initiative needs to be rolled out throughout the firm, covering both lawyers and support staff. All members of the firm need to understand, commit to and act and behave in accordance with the agreed values and culture.

(iv) Management of the initiative and progress on its implementation need to be a regular agenda item at the meetings of the most senior management group of the firm and be known to be so; clear endorsement by the senior decision-makers/management is critical.

(v) The implementation programme is likely to need to run for a number of years – not weeks or a few months. (In fact in some merged firms there is a sense that the programme only really starts to reach maturity when trainees who joined the firm post-merger become partners!). Ensuring all staff understand and are clear about the 'big picture' and act in accordance with achieving this and consistently with the firm values takes time.

Achieving behavioural change

For all staff, including partners, there is an inevitable focus on what the impact of the proposed merger is on each individual at a personal level. Irrespective of how powerful the rationale for merger is at the macro level, it is human nature that individuals will wish to understand what the implications are at a personal level and what is 'in it' for them. With more junior staff there is likely to be relatively little, if any, interest in and focus on the 'big picture' until they are satisfied with the consequences of merger at a personal level.

If there remain concerns at the personal level, be it among the most junior or most senior people, there will almost inevitably be a pursuit of personal agendas and behaviour more concerned with self-preservation than the overall development of the merged firm.

The dangers of overlooking this are substantial as is overlooking the general stress, uncertainty and turbulence created by merger.

In this context it is vitally important for those in management positions to remind themselves of the fact that while they will tend to be hugely committed to the merger – in part because of being architects to the merger and because of their involvement – the majority of others may be relatively ambivalent, significantly less convinced and interested by the 'macro' arguments and substantially more concerned by the anticipated impact on them individually.

It is therefore critical that through effective communication all staff – partners, lawyers and others – are aware of and understand the reason for the merger and similarly are aware of and understand the degree of change required in order for the objectives of the merged firm to be realised. Without a high level of awareness and understanding there is no realistic likelihood that people will contribute to the change required.

There is also a particular danger if the implementation of the activities required post-merger are taken for granted – it is assumed that they will just occur. Unfortunately such assumptions occur in far too many circumstances.

The post-merger integration has to be effectively planned, resourced and managed. It will not occur through desire alone. Behaviour consistent with the plan needs to be recognised and if appropriate incentivised and rewarded while behaviour inconsistent with or contrary to the plan cannot be tolerated.

In developing the plan it is vital to take into account the culture and values of each of the legacy firms and ignoring these is a high risk approach. Requiring people to do things that historically they have not done is likely to take them outside their comfort zone and this will result in all types of defensive behaviour. Equally, requiring people to operate in a more structured or managed environment is likely to meet with a defensive response if this is counter to what they have been used to in the past. Such 'negative' reactions can be significant if people have concerns about the merger or their future role in the merged firm and this is particularly likely to be the case if there is a perception that the previous levels of autonomy they have operated under are being eroded.

Achieving behavioural change is an enormous topic and again outside of the scope of this book. Clearly, however, having a high level of understanding across the merged firm of the reasons why the change is needed is key as is a sensitivity to the ways in which the required changes may run counter to the previous cultures in either of the legacy firms.

Lastly, it is important to recognise the magnitude of the required change and activities contained in the integration plan; breaking such plans into manageable chunks tends to be critical so that the implementation is not seen by people as overwhelmingly daunting; everything does not have to be achieved in the first week or month!

Business as usual

One, if not the most significant risk that merging firms face during both the pre- and in particular post-merger period is that partners and staff 'take their eyes off the ball' and become distracted by the merger and process of integration to the extent that clients perceive a deterioration in the quality of service received.

Ensuring that all staff remain 100% focused on providing exemplary levels of service to clients is absolutely critical and there are an increasing number of anecdotes in circulation concerning clients' perceptions of law firms becoming very inwardly focused during the pre- and post-merger period with the merger regarded as delivering two significant changes, both for the worse: a deterioration in service and an increase in fees!

Such anecdotes may not be wholly accurate but with them in circulation, merging firms have to be even more focused in ensuring that their clients neither experience nor perceive any such adverse events.

During the pre- and post-merger period, irrespective of any specific work related reasons, there is a strong rationale for a high level of contact with all core clients for as much as anything to demonstrate high levels of commitment to clients and client service.

Eight common aspects of post-merger integration plans

(i)   Achieving required partner performance

It may be that the expectations of partners in the merged firm are no different from the expectations of partners in each of the legacy firms, both in terms of the breadth of their roles and responsibilities and in terms of the levels of performance and contribution. This, however, is unlikely to be the case since if all partners in the merged firm continue working, performing and contributing in the same way as they have pre-merger nothing substantive is likely to change and all that will have been created is a larger firm.

The overall expectations of partners in the merged firm should be derived directly from the firm's strategic objectives and as well as clarifying contribution expectations in terms of performance should also establish the role and its breadth that partners are expected to fulfil.

Establishing certain aspects of the expectations of partners is relatively straightforward. If for example the new firm wishes to achieve profit per partner of say, £200,000 and anticipates achieving a profit margin of 30% then each partner needs to generate and manage on average a fee income of £666,666. Of course some partners will achieve more than this and some less but such calculations, albeit somewhat simplistic, do establish helpful norms.

Such norms can be taken to a further level of detail if that is considered helpful and be broken down to provide indications of the performance expectations of the partners themselves and the associates/assistants they delegate work to. For example, for the partner to achieve £200,000 in personal billings and delegate work to the value of the balance (£466,666) to three others who would each on average achieve personal billings of a little over £150,000.

The norms themselves can be taken to a further degree of detail in terms of chargeable hours, rates and recovery percentages and there is a decision again to be made as to whether such figures serve a useful purpose.

It needs to be stressed that there will of course be variations across the firm and different practice areas will be structured and operate according to market conditions. The norms should not be considered as a fixed target to which all must confirm but indicative. On the other hand it has to be accepted that if some partners contribute at a level 'below' these norms then other partners will need to contribute at a level correspondingly 'above' if the firm overall is to achieve its targets.

Establishing expectations of partners in other areas can also be developed although this can be more complicated.

It may be, for example, that the merged firm needs to focus particularly on business development targeted at certain types of clients or winning particular types of instruction. This might require partners to place a greater priority on business development than previously; some may relish such a challenge, others may find it a more daunting task. Again, however, expectations will need to be established and it may be appropriate for these to cover both levels of commitment (perhaps indicated in terms of committed hours) and levels of achievement (number of new clients and instructions won of a type consistent with the merged firm's objectives).

There may also be expectations covering for example delegation of work by partners to others and also the expectations of partners in terms of the training, development and coaching of others.

All ideally should be established in terms of unambiguous and specific expectations and targets so that all partners are clear of what is expected of them and equally can monitor and establish their progress towards achieving such targets.

If the expectations and targets are relatively stretching compared to the current expectations, either in terms of levels of performance or in terms of a significant broadening of the role or some combination of the two, then some or all partners may require support and assistance to achieve the new expectations.

Such support and assistance may be in terms of training to develop new capabilities. For example, in delegation or business development or, perhaps, in terms of more specific skills such as conference speaking or selling. Alternatively, or in addition, support and assistance may be required in terms of more general professional development in areas such as client management.

Ensuring partners have such skills and capabilities is critical because without them it is almost inevitable that the merged firm will not realise the objectives agreed.

Equally important and often more critical is providing support and assistance to partners to achieve the behavioural changes to bring their performance and contribution into line with expectations. Such support and assistance may be provided on a one-to-one individual basis or in a small group context or some combination of the two; this can be provided by internal staff or through the engagement of external consultants or through some combination of the two. Come what may, its primary role is to support, coach and encourage partners to perform in a way consistent with the achievement of the merged firm's strategic objectives.

Changes in behaviour particularly when they touch on fundamental aspects of working life (such as practising law less and delegating more or having to focus on marketing more extensively) are exceptionally hard to achieve and support and assistance can have a substantial impact. In some circumstances support and assistance to encourage and help partners develop new skills and achieve the necessary changes in performance is not required at all or if needed only in very specific focused areas; in other circumstances more extensive and widespread support and assistance may be required and this may need to continue over a period of time, albeit on a diminishing basis.

Of all issues to focus on post-merger, the issue of achieving partner behaviour and contribution in line with the strategic aims of the merged firms tends to be by far the most important and if insufficient attention is given to supporting and assisting the changes in behaviour consistent with the achievement of the strategic objectives of the merged firm, then the merged firm will inevitably fail to live up to its full potential.

Achieving such changes in behaviour and levels of performance is likely to be the most challenging issues post-merger. Creating an internal environment where partners (and others) do not feel threatened when trying and perhaps not always succeeding as they address new challenges is important, as is ensuring that there is not a stigma associated with not always being successful.

In this respect informal peer group support can be just as valuable as the more formal and structured support outlined above and other initiatives such as introducing an effective system to provide appraisal and feedback on performance can also be highly effective. (See following sections).

All of the above can, of course, be expensive both in financial and broader terms; the expense however of not committing to and developing and implementing a programme of partner support and assistance if this indeed is required is likely to be far greater; this, quite genuinely, is an investment not a cost.

(ii)   Achieving appropriate performance levels throughout the firm

Both at the start and end of the previous section there were specific references to levels of performance expected of partners.

The issue of achieving appropriate levels of performance consistent with the firm's underlying financial and business model has, of course, more extensive implications than merely focusing on the performance of partners.

In the discussions and negotiations leading up to merger, a budget for the new firm will have been produced and based on this, profitability forecasts will have been made; inevitably underpinning such forecasts will be assumptions on both costs (including any savings/increases that are a consequence of the merger) and fee income.

The fee income achieved will clearly be affected if the economic conditions under which the merged firm operates prove to be different from that forecast. If the conditions are more buoyant it will make it easier for the firm to achieve its forecasts, and, of course, vice versa. (The exception being if the firm has a substantially counter-cyclical practice focus).

As indicated previously, a failure to achieve forecast fee income in the first year of merger tends to be disappointing and almost inevitably demotivating and/or destabilising. Put another way:

achieving forecast fee income and profit targets is particularly important.

This requires a very strong concentration on operational performance in the year immediately proceeding merger and this should focus equally on financial results and client service. A focus on just the former can result in financial budgets being reached but client service and satisfaction falling, to the detriment of the merged firm in subsequent years. On the other hand a focus purely on client service can result in hugely satisfied clients but equally dissatisfied partners when profit expectations are not achieved.

Hence in the first year post-merger in particular, but almost as importantly in subsequent years, there needs to be a strong focus on operational performance as a top priority throughout the firm:

- identified potential cost savings need to be realised and while this can be particularly difficult if it involves redundancies to remove duplicate or superfluous staff, such difficulties tend not to get any easier to address if left for a year or so (and neither do they necessarily resolve themselves through a natural turnover in staff) and in the meantime the firm's competitiveness has been compromised by it carrying excess costs;
- uniform performance levels need to be established and lawyers managed so that these are achieved. For one or both legacy firm's lawyers these may be more demanding performance levels than historically expected. It is of course important that there is a single set of expectations covering all lawyers and that people are not working to their (differing) legacy firm expectations. If the differences between the expectations of the legacy firms are substantial there may need to be some transitional arrangements during which convergence is achieved, and, of course, there may be various employment law considerations to take into account if substantial changes are envisaged. In all this partners need to ensure that they are 'feeding' to associates, assistants and others sufficient work to allow them to achieve their chargeable hours performance expectations, although in other areas, such as commitment to marketing and business development it may be more up to each individual to be sufficiently self-motivated to commit to what is expected;
- establishing expected performance levels for support functions is also important to ensure that lawyers do have the levels and

responsiveness of back-up to allow them to fulfil their roles effectively. Such performance levels may in some circumstances be focused on specific, objectively measurable targets such as numbers of training programmes to be run, response times to notified systems failures, hours of marketing support committed to various practice areas, target dates for the production of month end financial accounts, and so on. In other cases the performance expectations will be of a more subjective nature.

Some of these performance expectations will be essentially firmwide (e.g. concerning lawyers' expected performance) while others will cover just certain groups of people or certain parts of the firm. Irrespective of this, what is critical is that:

(i)   the performance expectations are appropriate, realistic and unambiguous;
(ii) people understand them and commit to their achievement;
(iii) people have the skills, support and wherewithal to achieve the expected performance levels;
(iv) a clear plan is developed indicating how performance levels will be shifted from those existing pre-merger to those expected in the merged firm;
(v)   progress is managed and regularly assessed with appropriate action taken to address adverse variances.

(iii)   Roles, responsibilities, accountabilities and expectations of management

The roles and accountabilities of and the authority required by management in the merged firm may be very different from that of either or both legacy firms. If this is the case, this is an area that requires particular attention.

It may be that partners in one or both legacy firms have enjoyed relatively high levels of autonomy, perhaps both in terms of how they operate and the levels of commitment they choose to make. This type of environment may be quite counter to the requirements of the new firm.

Similarly one or both legacy firms may have been of a size (say up to 12–15 partners) where it has been feasible and felt appropriate to have significant partner involvement in most, if not all, decision making.

This is another area where significant change may be required post-merger with previous high levels of involvement in decision making no longer feasible, appropriate or effective due to, say, the increased size in terms of number of partners in the enlarged firm.

It is critically important that there is in circumstances such as these where for one or both firms there is a significant change in the style of management that there is clarity and understanding concerning what the changes are and their implications.

In particular it is important that there is understanding of and agreement to the roles, responsibilities, accountabilities and authorities of those in key management positions such as Senior Partner, Managing Partner, Head of Practice Area , lead client partners (see below) and so on. It is important also that there is a parallel level of clarity covering the business support directors for functions such as Accounts, HR, IT and Marketing.

It is equally important that there is clarity concerning the roles of the key management boards, particularly when there are a number, how they interact with one another, how they make and implement decisions and how they report back to the Partnership. And in this context it is important that should the involvement of partners in decision making from one or both legacy firms be significantly reduced that this too is understood.

Inevitably there will be hiccups and some initial problems because irrespective of how effective the initial planning and communication has been the new management will not work as effectively nor exactly as envisaged by everyone from the outset.

As a final point here it is important to have very effective communication from the outset from the various management groups to the Partnership (as owners of the business) and more widely in the firm so that people are kept properly informed about decisions, being consulted with in advance where appropriate.

It is through such communication that trust and confidence in the firm's management can be built and a greater likelihood that decisions, even if all not uniformly supported, are effectively implemented.

(iv)   Achieving practice group integration

Merging firms together will usually increase the number of partners and other lawyers working in each area of practice; the exception being when the two merging firms have no overlap in the services they offer and are entirely complementary in this respect; most likely two niche practices combining e.g. a contentious and non-contentious IP practice merging or a pensions practice with an employment firm.

The greater number of partners and lawyers working in each practice area will generate little additional competitiveness per se and this will be particularly the case if post-merger people continue providing services in pretty much the same way as they did in their legacy firms pre-merger and so clients experience no difference in the services they receive.

To improve competitiveness it is critical that the equivalent practice groups in each of the legacy firms achieve full integration and there are two reasons for this in particular:

(i) clients expect a high level of consistency from across a firm in the way that services are provided (we return to this point in the following section) and if each partner and lawyer continues to provide services in their own personal way consistency will not be achieved and clients will be less inclined to instruct others apart from the partner they already know; this instantly restricts the opportunities to cross-sell;

(ii) without practice group integration there will be little if any effective harnessing of the increased breadth and depth of expertise and capability and so while the size of the merged firm's practices will be larger, genuine critical mass and the competitive advantages that this can provide will not be realised.

In practice, achieving practice group integration involves ensuring common, uniform approaches to:

- how services are provided;
- quality management;
- client service protocols;
- knowledge management, development and sharing;
- precedent management and development;
- documentation;
- time recording;

- charge-out rates and charging (e.g. contingent and success fees);
- billing and invoicing;
- terms of business;
- risk management;
- business development, pitching and tendering;
- management and expectations of each level of staff (both fee earning and non-fee earning) within the framework of the firm's overall HR policies);
- individual career development, objective setting and performance appraisals (again within the framework of the firm's overall HR policies;
- training; etc.

Clearly this takes time to achieve and can also require considerable resource to achieve, particularly if the two legacy firms operated on a substantially different basis and/or had limited internal consistency prior to merging.

Given the fact that the overriding priority has to be on the provision of excellent levels of service to clients it can be a slow process before complete integration is achieved and as with other issues to address post-merger, a pragmatic approach based on prioritising needs to be pursued. Within this, however, achieving some 'early wins' is psychologically important in terms of building and maintaining commitment to integration and this will likely have some impact in establishing priorities.

(v)   Achieving a one firm style and approach

In parallel with achieving practice group integration (as outlined above) there is a need to achieve an overall, firmwide style and approach; this covers not only the behaviour and values that partners and other staff 'exhibit' but also the way that the firm operates more generally.

As indicated above clients expect to see a consistency in service from all parts of a firm (practices, offices and people). This does not mean there is an expectation of clone-like behaviour nor is there an expectation of the type and style of uniformity and consistency prevalent worldwide throughout, say, McDonald's. On the other hand there is an expectation of a level of consistency that is the instantly recognisable hallmark of the way the firm acts and provides services and is in someway unique to that firm.

At its heart it is concerned with the firm brand: not in terms of the portrayal of that in the corporate identity and related material although that is an integral and important aspect but in terms of the 'promise' that the firm explicitly or implicitly makes and the experience that clients have in comparison to that promise and their expectations when they instruct the firm. And if they are to be encouraged to instruct the firm widely it is critical that the experiences of using the different parts of the firm are consistent.

There are a number of dimensions to achieving this consistency in style and approach, but two in particular are central:

(i) The first concerns the attitudes and behaviour of people and the extent to which they deliver to the 'brand promise'. Are they, for example, genuinely client focused, responsive and commercial in their style and approach, delivering fully to client expectations that have been, at least in part, built up and shaped by the commitments the firm has made in its communications?

Of course each and every person in the firm will deliver on this promise to a greater or lesser extent in their own personal and unique way, fashioned at least to some extent by the job/role they are fulfilling. Nevertheless across every interaction that clients have with the myriad of people from within the firm that they interact with there needs to be a manifestation of the promise.

Clearly it takes time for this to permeate throughout the firm.

It needs those in leadership and management positions to act consistently as role models – be seen to be 'living' the promise in everything they do, each and every day. Development and training programmes can also play a major role to help ensure that a high level of understanding of the firm style and approach is achieved and maintained and that people do deliver on this on an ongoing basis.

Underpinning all of this, however, is the need for ongoing discussion and debate probably in both structured workshops and more informal ways of what the firm style and approach are and how these need to be 'lived'. And this all requires time and commitment.

Unfortunately many firms, both post-merger and independently of merger, take a rather different and high superficial approach to this issue. The Board or some other group takes itself away for a few hours or perhaps a weekend, possibly involving external facilitators, to discuss and agree the values, style and approach of the firm. These get written up in a paper and circulated to all partners and this pretty much is seen as the completion of the exercise. Hardly surprisingly this results in an essentially superficial outcome with no real level of understanding, commitment and buy-in and no focus on what these values, style and approach mean in practical terms and how people might 'deliver' against these.

All too often the outcome of exercises such as these is in effect no more than a series of words that typically include: Innovation, Service Excellence, Commerciality, Style and Spirit, etc., but no indication of what these mean in tangible terms and how people might deliver against them.

(ii) The second dimension concerns the more 'tangible' manifestations of the firm: the way services are provided, the style of the offices – or most certainly the reception and other public areas, and so on. Is there clear evidence, reinforced in each contact a client has with the firm, of a single consistent approach or is there more of a sense of eclecticism with each person and each office doing things in very much their own way?

Clearly there can be a major challenge in developing this consistency – partners from each of the legacy firms may historically have delivered services in very different ways and the merger may result in the firm operating from premises of a very differing nature. Lease or financial constraints may result in the merged firm having to continue to operate from differing premises for a considerable period of time post-merger and encouraging the behavioural changes to achieve a consistency in service delivery also takes time; this can be particularly the case in international mergers where there can be significant cultural differences impacting on the ways in which services are traditionally delivered.

Irrespective of such factors there is a requirement for merging firms to move as quickly as they can towards a one firm style and approach and this is best achieved through a properly planned and managed approach; just hoping that 'it' will occur is not a realistic strategy.

In this context bringing people from the merging firms into the same office or if post-merger the firm has more than one office in a location, mixing the people up has considerable merits. Similarly encouraging secondments and personnel moves between offices is highly worthwhile.

The aim clearly is for clients as quickly as possible to have forgotten that the firm is a result of merger and for it to be difficult or ideally impossible to identify which legacy firm each person in the merged firm originates from.

(vi) Developing a unified approach to client relationship management

In some respects developing a consistent approach to client relationship management is a 'sub-task' of the previous two issues (achieving practice group integration and a one firm style and approach). It is, however, an issue of such importance that it is worth treating in its own right as a post-merger integration issue.

As a rationale for the substantial majority of mergers there is a judgement that existing clients of one or both legacy firms could be better serviced by a larger, better resourced firm. In order to realise this clients will need to experience a consistency of service from people and practices within the merged firm. If the various people and practices provide services in very different ways there will be no motivation for clients to instruct the firm more extensively.

And this is where client relationship management comes in in terms of ensuring all parts of the firm that do or might provide services to a client genuinely understand the expectations of that client and deliver services in a way that not only meets those expectations but does so in a fashion that is superior to competitors.

Clearly some and most likely a large number of clients of each of the legacy firms will be relatively unaffected by the greater capabilities of the merged firm and for them 'service as normal' probably delivered through a single partner or a small team will remain the modus operandi.

For another group of clients, however, perhaps as few as 10–20 of the most significant clients of each legacy firm and most likely less than, say, 50 at a maximum, there will be a real opportunity to expand the breadth and depth of services provided. And it is on this small number, but of the most significant clients, that the merged firm needs to focus its client relationship management.

There are often twin aims concerning how work might be developed with these core clients: first in terms of breadth and volume of services provided and secondly in terms of winning an increasing share of a particular type of work – most often the higher value work.

It is important to consider on a client by client basis how this might be achieved and there is most certainly no 'one size fits all' approach. Having said this it is possible to identify certain characteristics that are common across the majority of successful CRM programmes:

- individual lead partners are appointed for each key client and they have both the responsibility and also the corresponding resources and authority to ensure the profitable development of each client;
- there is a clear reporting line from and acceptance of accountability to the firm's management (and ultimately the partnership) by each lead client partner;
- the firm's managements sets a high level of priority to the profitable development of the firm's core clients;
- each lead partner builds a core team to provide services to each core client and there is a high degree of stability in each team;
- from the lead partner and across the client team there is a very high level of commitment to the client's success – this in many circumstances is the differentiator between one firm and another and achieving and monitoring this requires considerable commitment;
- the mindset of each lead partner and team is not primarily focused on trying to provide an ever increasing range of services to the client and taking an increasing share of the client's wallet but on developing strong and enduring relationships of mutual benefit built on assisting clients achieve their long-term objectives and success;
- such relationships are built on a genuine depth of understanding of each client's business and the market sector within which they operate and based on this a pro-active approach to creating and

    delivering clear value to clients in the provision of services is implemented;

- development plans containing unambiguous aims and clear, measurable targets for each client are agreed and such plans contain tasks, actions and activities geared to ensure the achievement of such targets; implementation of the plans is effectively managed and achievement against plans is monitored both internally by the team and by the firm;
- all parts of the firm deliver services in a consistent way, tailored to the needs and expectations of the client and the lead partner has the authority to ensure this occurs;
- a mindset of the 'firm's clients' dominates.

Achieving a unified approach to client relationship management is again an issue that needs to be planned and managed rather than left to chance. It is likely to take several years to embed fully in the merged firm.

It can be especially difficult to achieve particularly if either or both legacy firms have not focused on this in the past and/or there is a high level of concern about the merger and partners are concerned or less than committed to expose what they see as 'their' clients to others, potentially leading to them having a less strong relationship with such clients as a consequence. This can be a particular issue if partners see such clients as 'their' following, possibly as an entrée and to take to another firm should they decide to move on.

(vii) Developing and implementing an effective programme of strategically targeted new business development

A strategic aim of the majority of mergers is to attract new clients to the merged firm that neither legacy firm had the capability, capacity, credibility or competitiveness to attract previously.

Assuming that the appropriate merger has been undertaken the combined firm should be well positioned to attract such clients but it is vital to recognise that in the main such clients will not come beating a path to the door but will have to be converted from prospects to profitable clients by means of a targeted and focused business development programme; it is likely to be a long and most likely indefinite wait for the telephone to start ringing otherwise.

A targeted programme of business development needs to be developed, committed to and implemented; this needs to be an ongoing programme of activities, not something that will operate for only a limited time post-merger.

It needs to have the full support of the senior management of the firm, be properly resourced and effectively managed with clear responsibilities, accountabilities and roles allocated.

It may, of course, be appropriate to encourage partners to continue with their more personal business development activities and some of this is likely to be 'structured' while other aspects will be more 'opportunistic'. These activities, however, are not necessarily going to bring to the firm the type of clients and work that is really wanted. It may be profitable and interesting work but not necessarily of the type consistent with the strategic aims; alternatively it may be work of the type wanted but not from the desired clients or conversely from the desired client type but not of the desired work type.

Only a targeted business development programme has a high degree of likelihood of bringing in both the type of client and type of work wanted and hence having such a programme in place and effectively implemented needs to be a priority.

The nature, style and magnitude of such a programme will be dependent on the circumstances the merged firm faces and the extent to which it needs to develop its client base in order to achieve its strategic objectives: it might be a relatively modest programme or something more extensive.

A key issue in many circumstances is that the merged firm is seeking to build a client base that comprises higher quality, more prestigious, larger and more sophisticated clients than the legacy firms tended to act for in the main in the past.

This will require partners to target client organisations that are outside their previous experience. Some partners will be enthusiastic and rise to this challenge; others, and more likely than not the majority, will be hesitant, nervous or somewhat lacking in confidence in undertaking such activities. It will be requiring them to work outside their 'comfort zone' and this can be difficult to achieve.

Clearly there is a logic in utilising the merged firm's best 'rainmakers' to play a leading role in any business development programme but there tends to be a need to bring in a wider range of partners and hence encouraging at least some partners to operate outside their comfort zone becomes essential.

Getting partners to work in teams is one way of achieving this, as is providing support, training and development; one-to-one coaching and mentoring can also be effective.

Providing high level supporting analysis and information on the targeted clients and their market sectors can also assist as can providing assistance with preparing marketing events and literature.

Ultimately, however, what needs to occur is for designated partners to make contact with identified prospective clients and start the process of converting such prospects into profitable clients of the firm.

It is worth making two final points in this respect:

(i)   new client wins tend to have a very significant psychological impact and hence although there may be a huge range of demands on people's time in the period post-merger maintaining business development as a high priority is important;

(ii) in business development activities it is important that these involved do not over promise in terms of what the newly merged firm can deliver. 'Seamless service' between offices and practice groups is not likely to be achieved from the outset and it would be a mistake to raise client expectations in this respect to unrealistic levels. As indicated above new client wins deliver a particularly strong psychological boost to newly merged firms; subsequently losing such clients shortly later through failing to deliver to the expectations of those clients has an equally demoralising and negative impact.

(viii)   Developing and implementing uniform HR policies

In some circumstances it is possible to establish common HR policies covering all HR issues prior to merger; this however tends to be relatively rare. More common is to address the HR issues that have to be addressed pre-merger and 'park' other issues, leaving them to be dealt with post-merger.

On this basis HR issues related to 'Terms and Conditions' tend to be the focus of the pre-merger period, with other issues such as training and development, appraisals, career progression and even partner admission criteria and procedures left until post-merger.

On 'Terms and Conditions', some firms merging achieve agreement on a common approach prior to merger. This can be relatively straightforward if the legacy firms are similar in the approach. Achieving agreement on a common approach can also usually be relatively easily achieved if the merged firm is prepared to adopt the most 'generous' approach (from the employees' perspective) of the legacy firms' policies on each aspect of 'Terms and Conditions': this as indicated earlier can be a very expensive approach and may also result in terms and conditions that are not consistent with the requirements of the merged firm and its strategic objectives (e.g. core office hours, periods of continuous holiday allowed, and so on).

Clearly if the merger is going to result in staff from the legacy firms working alongside each other in the same office from the outset there will almost inevitably be difficulties if such staff's terms and conditions are not broadly equivalent and ideally identical.

Many mergers, of course, do not result in staff from the legacy firms working in the same offices – the chances are they may be in separate cities or even countries. In such circumstances the need to have similar or even identical terms and conditions is likely to be reduced and possibly even nonexistent. Differences in costs of living, market conditions and local practice can legitimately justify differences in terms and conditions and potentially on an ongoing basis. (Secondments between offices can then create some challenges but these are not normally insuperable).

For many merging firms the approach taken on terms and conditions tends to be one of achieving convergence over a period of time on at least most issues: neither going for completely common terms and conditions on Day 1 nor planning to operate with radically differing terms and conditions indefinitely.

Such an approach can defer some of the costs that would be incurred under the 'most generous approach' outlined above and also provides some breathing space to develop new terms and conditions that are aligned with and supportive of the achievement of the strategic aims of the merged firm.

Achieving a common approach on HR issues tends to be better done sooner rather than later but this is an area that probably can be deferred if resource constraints and other priorities dictate that this has to occur.

HR matters such as recruitment, training and development, staff supervision, career progression and so on should each be addressed from the perspective of the needs of the merged firm, the market position it is trying to occupy and the strategy it is pursuing. If on these factors the merged firm is very different from both of the legacy firms, there is a strong likelihood that the HR policies of neither firm will be particularly suitable for the merged firm to adopt – they will be inconsistent with the needs of the merged firm.

In these circumstances it is clearly appropriate to develop entirely new HR policies although 'borrowing' where sensible aspects of the HR policies of either or both of the legacy firms.

An advantage of developing new HR policies is that it avoids any sense of 'imposition' by one firm on the other and reinforces the sense of a 'fresh' start with a new and different approach.

In practice what tends to occur in many mergers is that one or other firm to the merger will have more developed and effective HR policies and these will largely form the basis of the HR policies for the merged firm.

As a final comment on this point the development of HR policies for the merged firm can provide excellent opportunities for people at various levels from the merging firms to work together influencing the 'shape' and 'feel' of the new firm and this tends to be worth taking advantage of.

Concluding considerations

Achieving effective post-merger integration is absolutely critical, it has to be regarded as a priority and resourced and managed accordingly. Post-merger integration needs to be properly planned and that plan driven through to implementation.

Senior level partner commitment is critical and this may necessitate one or more partners having a significant or even full-time responsibility for ensuring plans are implemented and progress in line with these achieved.

The better the pre-merger planning and due diligence the less likely that unexpected factors will arise in the post-merger integration and in this respect particular attention to differences in culture between the two firms is important. Irrespective, however, of the thoroughness of the pre-merger planning and due diligence unexpected factors and hurdles will emerge.

And at the root of many of the difficulties in post-merger integration is the fact that irrespective of how compelling the business case for merger is and how much partners (and others) like the idea of merger behavioural change is extraordinarily difficult to achieve.

Given this, it is critical that the merged firm does not over promise: neither internally nor to clients and the market in terms of what it will deliver.

Both partners and staff and clients will tend to have high expectations of the merged firm and it is critical that these are not raised still further. From within the firm there is likely to be an expectation that the shortcomings and irritations of the legacy firms will (miraculously) disappear overnight; unfortunately such expectations are never met. Clients, meanwhile, are likely to have raised expectations of the merged firm: in part because the merged firm is likely to have raised such expectations in its communication with clients and in part because clients tend implicitly to assume that a larger, better resourced firm will provide superior levels of service.

In practice any such changes to levels of service do not occur at the outset of a merger and it is more likely than not that 'glitches' in service will occur. And, of course, any other service shortcomings, even if they have occurred quite independently of merger are likely as not to be perceived to be a consequence of the merger.

Hence it is critical to be open and honest with clients. It is generally best to be direct in acknowledging that the benefits of merger will not all 'flow through' immediately and that from time to time service shortcomings may occur. In this context seeking clients' input on how things might be improved and encouraging them to make contact when service is off the mark are both sound approaches.

It is invariably better in the long run to follow such a path rather than to promise clients more than can realistically be delivered, raising their expectations as a consequence and then failing to come close to delivering. The consequences of this are virtually inevitable in terms of lost trust, confidence and clients.

As a final point it is critical that newly merged firms maintain a very high level of external focus throughout the post-merger integration period. Inevitably achieving post-merger integration results in a great number of internal initiatives being pursued. In parallel there is an almost inevitable focus to a greater or lesser extent on 'internal politics'. The real danger however is that clients experience or perceive a decline in service as a consequence. And this must be avoided at all costs. Clients must experience a continuous sense of being at the centre of the merged firm's and all its staff's attention.

Appendices

Appendix I – Initial Meeting Agenda

Objective of meeting

The primary purpose of the meeting is to:

(i)   explore in outline the strength of the business rationale for merger;
(ii) consider issues that might prevent a merger taking place;
(iii) establish whether further meetings/exchange of information would be worthwhile.

Agenda

1. Brief overview of each firm:

   - History and current position
   - Primary strategic aims
   - Client base
   - Practice area capabilities
   - Geographic capabilities
   - Leadership and management structure
   - Internal environment, values, culture

2. Level of overlap/complementarity of strategic aims of each firm in terms of their desired future market positions, both nationally and internationally in, say, 3–5 years and including:

   - core client types
   - core practice areas
   - value focus (high, medium, low)
   - basis of competitiveness
   - geographical locations

3. What are the potential 'show stoppers' (i.e. issues that both firms feel strongly about and would prefer to retain what they have).

4. Discussion, in broad terms, about each firm's expectations in regard to:

   - the role of management and management structure (including practice group management);
   - the role of partners (including performance expectations);

- profit sharing (including drawings policies);
- partnership structure (single or multiple tier);
- approaches to financing the business (e.g. borrowing policies, etc.);
- style of working (team based or essentially individual);
- approach to client relationship management and business development;
- relationship between fee earning and support departments.

5. The 'shape' of the economics of the 'New Firm' in say 3 to 5 years:

- likely fee income;
- likely cost base, with an emphasis on both the costs of merger and post-merger integration and identifiable potential cost savings;
- desired profit margin and profit per partner.

6. Initial assessment of the strength of the business case based on above:

- agree on next steps' issues for discussion and/or additional exchange of information.

Appendix II – Assessment Criteria Framework

The following criteria will provide a useful framework for assessing each firm and ultimately identifying the preferred firm:

1. Overlap/complementarity of strategies.
2. Potential to improve competitiveness.
3. Identified synergies between main practice areas.
4. Approach to quality management.
5. Extent to which there is a compatible culture and style of working.
6. Extent to which internal environment is compatible.
7. Performance expectations of individuals.
8. Overall approach to management.
9. Extent of international outlook and commitment to building an international capability (if relevant).
10. Compatibility of people.

Appendix III – Firm Profile Indicative Framework

Introduction	History, size, culture
Strategy and Development	Strategic aims and actions to achieve these
Structure and Size	Fee earner numbers, grade, age profile, leverage
Financial Performance	Data supported by text including forward projections
Premises	Office locations and leases
Major Practice Areas	Work types, principal clients
Directory Rankings	Legal directories (or equivalent)
Transaction Activity	Transaction databases
Recent Significant Matters	c.1 page per practice area
Partnership Remuneration	Structure, years to plateau, points range, criteria
Management Structure and Governance	Structure, roles, responsibilities, reporting lines
Internal Environment	Culture, behaviour, work processes

Appendix IV – Proposed Agenda for Follow-Up Meetings with Shortlisted Firms

1. Strategy
   - to confirm that the strategic aims of the two firms are consistent/ complementary
   - to ensure that each firm has similar aims in terms of what might be achieved through merger.

2. Business Case
   - to consider the strength of the business case based on analysis/ discussion around the client base, practice areas and economic structure of the two firms
   - to identify potential client and prospect opportunities (and conflicts)
   - to review the competitiveness of a combined firm alongside competitor practices
   - to identify and assess strategic gains achievable
   - to discuss whether such gains might be achievable through an alliance.

3. Review current status in each firm on key matters, identifying potential hurdles/issues in integrating
   - capital structure and borrowings policy
   - equity partner reward system and drawings policy
   - equity partner status, rewards and position
   - non-equity partner status, rights, position in regard to equity and rewards
   - partner selection/promotion criteria
   - management structure including role, responsibility definitions, accountability
   - decision making structure
   - management processes
   - details of central services/administration

4. Timing

- to determine if the preferred timing is realistic/feasible
- to establish programme for addressing issues to be resolved:
  - Partnership Deed
  - Management Structure
  - Remuneration and Profit Sharing
  - Financial and Accounting Integration
  - Financial Due Diligence
  - Client Due Diligence/Conflict
  - HR Policies
  - IT Integration
  - Marketing Integration
  - Transitional Arrangements
  - Launch Plans

Appendix V – Outline Business Case

1. Introduction
2. Strategic objectives of the two firms
3. Immediate impact of merger/shape of combined firm
4. Competitive/market trends
5. Assessment of enhanced competitiveness of combined firm
6. Opportunities created by merger (existing clients/referrers; new clients/ referrers; internal efficiency/effectiveness)
7. Financial considerations including turnover/profitability trends of each Firm
8. International reach/aims
9. Summary; feasibility of merger; timetable
10. Critical success factors

Appendix

1. Overview of each Firm

- 'The firm at a glance'
- Salient characteristics
- Partnership, management and organisational structure
- Culture
- Partner compensation/drawings policy
- Capital/financing/contingent liabilities and future financial obligations
- Infrastructure systems and applications

2. Overview of major practice areas of each firm
3. Core client base of each firm
4. Identified conflicts

Appendix VI – Practice Group Meeting Agenda

The primary purpose of these meetings is for Partners to gain an understanding of the Practice Group post-merger and to begin planning what they will do to develop and grow the business.

1. Core clients (type of work; fee income; client partners)
2. Main types of work carried out in the Practice Group
3. Fee earner structure
   – particular strengths of each fee earner
4. Sources of work in the past
   – referrals
   – on-going clients
5. Administrative support to the Group (e.g. Finance, Training, Marketing etc.)
6. Economics (including chargeable hours per fee earner by category, hourly rates, realisation percentage etc.)
7. HR policies within the Group including training, mentoring/coaching, quality control and social activities
   – if available detail of what is expected of each category of fee earner
8. Identification of existing clients where opportunities exist for the new Group
   – outline action plan per client
9. Staff gaps and plans to close these
10. Potential new clients that could be pursued
11. Opportunities with clients of other Groups
12. What can be done to increase competitiveness
13. Outline plan for first year and subsequent years post-merger
14. Actions required over first six months to achieve integration within the Group

Appendix VII – Master Work Plan

(i)   Partnership Deed

- **Primary Output:**   A new Partnership Deed reflecting the requirements of the new firm.
- **Dependencies:**   Brief from Steering Committee.
- **Completion Date**

(ii)   Partner Profit Sharing

- **Primary Output:**   The proposed profit sharing system; the position of Partners in that system for the year of merger and subsequent years (where predictable).
- **Dependencies:**   Performance assessment of Partners.
- **Completion Date**

(iii)   Financial and Accounting

- **Primary Output:**   Financial policies for the new firm; due diligence on the two existing firms; proposals to deal with difficult issues; process for integrating systems; outline budget for year of merger and subsequent years.
- **Dependencies:**   Profitability projections
- **Completion Date**

(iv)   Client Due Diligence (including Conflict Checks)

- **Primary Output:**   Feedback from core clients regarding proposed merger; clients where professional or commercial conflicts exist or potentially exist; a process for checking client conflicts on an ongoing basis.
- **Dependencies:**   Nil.
- **Completion Date**

(v)   Human Resource Policies

- **Primary Output:**   A proposed HR policy/strategy for the merged firms dealing with all critical areas of HR management; proposals to deal with areas where there are differences between the two firms; proposals to ensure the transition period handles HR issues effectively.
- **Dependencies:**   Practice Group Heads.
- **Completion Date**

(vi)   Technology

- **Primary Output:**   An outline plan for technology development within the merged firm plus a top level budget; a plan and budget for the integration of technology practices and systems.
- **Dependencies:**   Practice Group Heads.
- **Completion Date**

(vii)   Marketing Policies

- **Primary Output:**   An outline marketing plan for the merged firm along with a top level budget; a plan for integrating the marketing functions of the two firms.
- **Dependencies:**   Practice Group Heads.
- **Completion Date**

(viii)   Premises & Facilities

- **Primary Output:**   A plan that ensures the offices of the new firm operate effectively and efficiently and that the potential cost savings over the next, say, three years are optimised.
- **Dependencies:**   Practice Group Heads.
- **Completion Date**

Appendix VIII – Communications Checklist

I. Preparatory steps

i.   If media consultant will be used, notify as early as possible, well before scheduled announcement date.
ii. Draw up contingency plan in case word leaks out (as it often does).
iii. Emphasise to all parties the importance of secrecy.
iv. Select PR contacts.

- One for each firm
- One for each branch office (vis-à-vis local media)
- Backups for each

v.   Prepare plan.

- Date for notification of key clients
- Date for notification of all clients
- Dates for notification of all partners, associates, and staff
- Date for press release

vi.   Prepare fact sheet and approve contents.
vii. Prepare press release(s) and have approved.
viii. Prepare information package., contents to include:

- Senior partner introduction
- Fact sheet
- Press release
- Firm brochures and other promotional material
- Published articles about the firms
- Distribution: Clients, press, firm members, others

II. Informing clients

i.   Prepare information for client relationship partners.

- Benefits to clients
- Typical client concerns, questions and answers

ii.   Prepare for meetings with clients.

- Which clients, partners and when to occur
- Need for confidentiality

iii.   Prepare for calls to clients.

- Which clients, partners and when to occur
- Need for confidentiality

iv.   Prepare letters to clients.

- Mailing list, date of mailing
- Common content: Benefits to clients; client concerns to address or to be addressed. Information on other firm (brochure, published articles, etc.) and/or fact sheet and/or press release
- Varied content: Each firm; different types of clients
- Approval, signature (managing partner, billing partner, or responsible lawyer)

III.   Informing the press

i.   Prepare a 'Holding Statement' for any speculative press enquiries (see Appendix IX)
ii.   Prepare a plan for contacting press.

- Simultaneous release or other approach
- Media to contact personally and by whom: national general press, national business press, national legal press, local general media, local business press, relevant trade publications (vis-à-vis practice specialties)
- Possible press questions
- Answers for possible press questions

iii.   Prepare press list for blanket distribution of press release.

IV.   Internal communications

i.   Prepare memo to lawyers and staff.

- Official spokespersons
- Official information they can divulge if asked

ii.   Determine if any meetings are necessary.

V.   Communication Events to consider

i.   Plan press conference.

- Lawyers preparation
- Date and place
- Plan for contacting media

ii.   Plan social events (open houses, seminars, etc., to introduce clients to new partners).

iii.   Prepare tombstone ads.

- Text
- Publications in which they will appear
- Typesetting

Appendix IX – Press Holding Statement

Prior to any formal press release, both firms need to be prepared to respond to any speculative enquires.

If an enquiry is received from the press prior to any formal announcement the likelihood is that:

(i) any contact from the press is a consequence of them having some sort of information that discussions are taking place;
(ii) if the press does contact one firm it will also contact the other.

Hence an outright denial is unlikely to be an appropriate response and consistency between what the two firms say is important.

It is important to develop in advance a ' holding statement' response for each firm. An identical 'holding statement' from both firms will almost certainly fuel speculation and so each firm should develop its own statement, based on the following factors as appropriate:

- highly competitive, rapidly evolving market;
- clients' needs and expectations constantly evolving;
- need for all firms that wish to remain successful to continuously review their competitiveness and future options;
- as part of this, inevitably keep in touch with similarly focused firms;
- in this context have had discussions from time to time with Firm X, but are not currently in formal merger discussions with them or indeed any firm.

Should either firm get such an enquiry, it is vital that the other firm be notified immediately. We also recommend that each firm nominates a partner (and a back-up) to handle such enquiries.

All partners should be informed of these procedures and also be aware of the response given to any press enquiries.

Appendix X – Typical Press Questions

1. Why are the firms merging/considering merger?
2. Isn't this really an acquisition?
3. Is either firm in any financial or other difficulty?
4. Who suggested merger first?
5. How did the discussions come about?
6. Where will the firm be based?
7. Will the firm drop or add any offices?
8. Will any lawyers be leaving either firm? If so, why?
9. Will all current partners remain partners?
10. Will any lawyers be transferred to other offices?
11. Do the firms have different tracks to partnership? If so, how will differences be resolved?
12. Who will run the new firm?
13. What will the management structure be?
14. Have or will any clients be lost for conflict reasons?
15. Will any clients leave either firm as a result of the merger?
16. Are there any plans for further expansion?
17. What kinds of clients will the new firm be targeting?
18. What are annual billings for each firm?
19. What are anticipated billings for the merged firm?
20. How will a name be chosen?
21. What are the contentious issues of negotiations?
22. Have they all been resolved?
23. Has either firm had any significant defections recently? If so, was that a factor in the merger?

Appendix XI – Public Relations Information Checklist

I. Existing firms (one for each firm)

i. Main contact person for press
ii. Backup contact
iii. Office locations (addresses and telephone numbers)
iv. Number of partners, associates, paralegals, and staff
v. Relative size of firm in a relevant geographical area (e.g., 'the largest firm in city')
vi. Characterisation of firm (e.g., 'a full-service firm with specialties or concentrations in telecommunications, competition and trade regulation, and tax')
vii. Other substantial practice areas not mentioned as specialties above
viii. Notable lawyers in firm
ix. Major clients who would not object to being listed
x. Names of any mergers over past five years, number of lawyers in each, when took place, etc.
xi. Notable accomplishments (e.g., major cases or transactions)
xii. Other relevant information of potential interest

II. New firm

i. Name
ii. Reason for merger
iii. Number of partners, associates, paralegals, and staff
iv. Offices that will be added or combined or changes in location
v. Relative size of firm (e.g., 'will make the firm the largest in city, region').
vi. Characterisation (e.g., 'a full-service firm specialising in ...')
vii. Major practice areas not mentioned above (in approximate order of importance)
viii. Plans for further expansion
ix. Other significant changes
x. Date of merger vote
xi. Date merger becomes effective
xii. Management structure
xiii. Key management members and their positions
xiv. Lawyers who will be leaving and why (if appropriate)
xv. Lawyers making or losing partnership (if appropriate)

xvi. Lawyers who will be transferred to other offices
xvii. Notable lawyers
xviii. Firm's major target client types (e.g., large corporations, high-tech firms, investment banks)
xiv. Major clients who would not object to being listed
xx. Clients that firm will lose as a result of merger and why (if appropriate)

Appendix XII – Plan for Financial Integration – Checklist

1. Forecast projections for year 1 (including revenue, costs, cash flow).
2. Tax (and legal) aspects of alternative methods of combination.
3. Determine liabilities and debt.
4. Proposed capital structure.
5. Proposed capital and borrowings policies.
6. Financial system integration/migration to single system.
7. Professional liability cover.
8. Billing and collections policies (include contingent fee arrangements, pro-bono).
9. Appointment of external accountants/auditors.
10. Performance expectations (including hours, rates, etc.).
11. Balance sheet consolidation.
12. Structure and staffing of Accounts Department (include transitional arrangements).

Index